555 Reasons to Roll Your Eyes at American Politics

Your Great Big Grab Bag of Useless Helpful Tidbits

Michael Clutton and Michael P. Clutton

Published by Michael Clutton, 2024.

555 REASONS TO ROLL YOUR EYES AT AMERICAN POLITICS

First edition. July 2, 2024.

ISBN: 979-8227081735

Written by Michael Clutton and Michael P. Clutton.

Table of Contents

555 Reasons to Roll Your Eyes at American Politics

American politics is a fascinating spectacle, a grand theatre where local governance and national aspirations collide in a whirlwind of policies, personalities, and power plays. From the humble city council meetings that decide where the new stop sign goes to the high-stakes drama of presidential elections that grip the nation and the world, American politics is a complex and multifaceted beast.

The American political system is designed to balance power, prevent tyranny, and ensure representation. It's an intricate dance between the federal and state governments, a tug-of-war between different branches of government, and a never-ending battle of ideologies. Whether you're a political junkie or just trying to make sense of the latest headlines, understanding this system is crucial for anyone navigating or merely observing the political landscape.

American politics affects every aspect of life, from the taxes we pay to the roads we drive on, the education our children receive, and the air we breathe. It shapes the laws governing our society, the rights we enjoy, and our duties to our fellow citizens. In this ever-evolving arena, the stakes are high, and the outcomes can be profound, making it essential to grasp the significance and mechanics of American politics.

What's the Point?

"Your Great Big Grab Bag of Useless Helpful Tidbits: 555 Reasons to Roll Your Eyes at American Politics" takes you through American politics' zany, bewildering, and often absurd world. This book is not your typical civics lesson; it's a delightful mix of practical insights and entertaining tidbits that will leave you both informed and amused.

Think of this book as your political tour guide, leading you through a labyrinth of historical anecdotes, quirky facts, and surprising truths about the system that governs the United States. Whether waiting for your coffee to brew or hiding from your in-laws, this book provides the perfect escape into political trivia and humorous observations.

We're here to explore the oddities and intricacies of American politics, from the founding fathers' grand experiments to the modern-day media circus.

Along the way, you'll encounter everything from presidential pets to bizarre election outcomes, and yes, even why candidates spend tens of millions campaigning for jobs that pay less than two hundred grand. With a light-hearted and engaging approach, we aim to inform, entertain, and perhaps make you scratch your head between laughs. So, grab your popcorn—this is American politics like you've never seen it before!

Chapter 1: The Foundations of American Politics

The Great Debate Over... Seating Arrangements?

Picture this: It's the sweltering summer of 1787 in Philadelphia, and the Constitutional Convention is in full swing. Founding Fathers are packed into a room, fanning themselves with their hats and discussing the future of a nation. But before they could even get to the heavy stuff—like, you know, writing the Constitution—they had a heated debate over something far more critical: where everyone would sit.

Before debating federalism, the balance of powers, or individual rights, the delegates spent much time squabbling over seating arrangements. Should it be alphabetical by state? Should the larger states sit up front? Maybe a random draw from a powdered wig? Eventually, they settled on a method that seemed fair enough: alphabetical by state. This way, at least, no one could claim the New Yorkers were too close to the refreshments or that the Virginians were hogging all the good seats.

It's comforting to know that even the creators of one of the most significant documents in history were not immune to the timeless human need to argue about seating arrangements.

Grab Bag of Useless Helpful Tidbits

Useless Helpful Tidbit 1: James Madison, often called the "Father of the Constitution," was relatively small. Standing at about 5'4", he proves that great things can come in small packages.

Useless Helpful Tidbit 2: The Federalist Papers were initially published anonymously under the pseudonym "Publius." Today, they'd probably just be another anonymous Twitter thread.

Useless Helpful Tidbit 3: Rhode Island was the only state that refused to send delegates to the Constitutional Convention. They had better things to do, like holding the country's first recorded chicken dance contest.

Useless Helpful Tidbit 4: The original Constitution did not include the Bill of Rights. These ten amendments were added later after much insistence from those who wanted to avoid a sequel convention.

Useless Helpful Tidbit 5: Benjamin Franklin, the oldest delegate at the Convention, often had to be carried to the sessions in a sedan chair due to his poor health. Talk about making an entrance.

Useless Helpful Tidbit 6: George Washington, presiding over the Convention, hardly ever spoke during the proceedings. When he did, everyone listened—like when the boss finally chimes in on a heated email thread.

Useless Helpful Tidbit 7: The phrase "We the People" was a late addition to the Preamble. It beat out the less catchy "We the States" and the even more cumbersome "We the Guys Who Are Sick of Arguing."

Useless Helpful Tidbit 8: The Constitution was signed on September 17, 1787, but it took almost a year for enough states to ratify it. If you think waiting for your Amazon package is tough, try waiting for national consensus.

Useless Helpful Tidbit 9: The phrase "We the People" was a late addition to the Preamble. It beat out the less catchy "We the States" and the even more cumbersome "We the Guys Who Are Sick of Arguing."

Useless Helpful Tidbit 10: The Constitution was signed on September 17, 1787, but it took almost a year for enough states to ratify it. If you think waiting for your Amazon package is tough, try waiting for national consensus.

Useless Helpful Tidbit 11: Alexander Hamilton proposed that the President and Senators serve for life. His idea was politely declined, which is a founding-era way of saying, "Get real, Alex."

Useless Helpful Tidbit 12: The Constitutional Convention was held secretly, with windows nailed shut to prevent eavesdropping. This secrecy might explain why the room was so darn hot.

Useless Helpful Tidbit 13: John Adams and Thomas Jefferson were abroad during the Constitutional Convention. Adams tried to avoid tea in England, and Jefferson was in France, perfecting his wine palate.

Useless Helpful Tidbit 14: The two-party system we know today wasn't in the original design. The Founding Fathers had hoped for a government free of partisan divides—ah, sweet, naive optimism.

Useless Helpful Tidbit 15: The "necessary and proper" clause, also known as the elastic clause, was included to allow Congress to pass laws needed to carry out their powers. Think of it as the original "fine print."

Useless Helpful Tidbit 16: The Constitution originally stated that only free persons (excluding Native Americans) would be counted for representation. This would later be amended, but not without significant strife and conflict.

Useless Helpful Tidbit 17: Gouverneur Morris, credited with writing the Preamble, had a wooden leg due to a carriage accident. He didn't let that slow him down when crafting some of the most enduring words in American history.

Useless Helpful Tidbit 18: The original Constitution did not mention political parties. The framers envisioned a government united in purpose. They hadn't spent much time on Facebook.

Useless Helpful Tidbit 19: The delegates worked in sweltering conditions with all windows shut for secrecy, which made the convention smell like a gym locker room by the end of summer.

Useless Helpful Tidbit 20: Despite the intense debates and differing opinions, the delegates kept their sense of humor, occasionally breaking into song or playful banter to lighten the mood.

Great Big Grab Bag of Fun Factoids

Fun Factoid 1: Only 39 of the 55 delegates at the Constitutional Convention signed the final document. The rest either refused or had already left Philadelphia in a huff.

Fun Factoid 2: The Federalist Papers, advocating for the ratification of the Constitution, were written in just under a year by Alexander Hamilton, James Madison, and John Jay. They were the colonial version of binge-writing.

Fun Factoid 3: George Washington was unanimously elected president of the Constitutional Convention, a rare feat that makes modern political unanimity look like a fairy tale.

Fun Factoid 4: The Constitutional Convention lasted from May 25 to September 17, 1787. By the end, many delegates were so tired of debating that they were willing to sign almost anything just to go home.

Fun Factoid 5: The original Constitution is housed at the National Archives in Washington, D.C., where it's kept in a bulletproof case filled with argon gas. Talk about a high-maintenance document.

Chapter 2: The Electoral Process

The Case of the Disappearing Campaign

In the election of 1872, things took a rather unusual turn. Horace Greeley, the editor of the New York Tribune, ran against incumbent Ulysses S. Grant. Greeley's campaign was peculiar from the start, marked by his erratic speeches and unconventional views. As a newspaper editor, Greeley had been a vocal critic of the Grant administration, but his transition from journalist to presidential candidate was fraught with challenges. His speeches were often rambling, and his platform, which included advocating for vegetarianism and opposing smoking, bewildered many voters.

Grant won by a landslide, securing his second term in office with relative ease. However, the story didn't end there. Shortly after the election, Greeley's health began to deteriorate rapidly. Overwhelmed by the stress of the campaign and the loss, Greeley passed away just weeks after the voting on November 29, 1872. This tragic turn led to a peculiar situation in the Electoral College.

Greeley had won 66 electoral votes, but since he was deceased, those votes could not be officially cast for him. Consequently, his electoral votes were scattered among various other candidates, including Thomas Hendricks, Charles Jenkins, and David Davis—this scattering of votes added to the confusion and oddity of the 1872 election outcome.

The bizarre nature of Greeley's campaign and its aftermath left a lasting impression on American electoral history. His run for the presidency, which had started with high hopes and a considerable following, ended most unusually and tragically. The scattering of his electoral votes underscored the complexities and unforeseen events that can arise in the electoral process.

Greeley's campaign became a ghost, disappearing almost as quickly as it had emerged, leaving behind a strange and somber footnote in the annals of American politics. The 1872 election serves as a reminder of the unpredictable nature of political life and the personal toll it can take on those who dare to enter the fray.

Grab Bag of Useless Helpful Tidbits

Useless Helpful Tidbit 1: The Electoral College was established as a compromise between electing the president by a vote in Congress and by popular vote of citizens. Essentially, it's a system designed to please everyone and no one at the same time.

Useless Helpful Tidbit 2: In the early days, electors would cast two votes each for president, with the runner-up becoming vice president. This led to the awkward situation of having President John Adams and Vice President Thomas Jefferson, who were political rivals and didn't quite see eye to eye.

Useless Helpful Tidbit 3: The shortest presidential campaign in U.S. history was that of William Henry Harrison in 1840. His campaign slogan, "Tippecanoe and Tyler Too," was longer than his presidency, which lasted only 31 days due to his untimely death.

Useless Helpful Tidbit 4: The election of 1824 was decided by the House of Representatives after none of the candidates secured a majority of the electoral votes. John Quincy Adams was eventually declared the winner, much to the chagrin of Andrew Jackson, who had won the popular vote.

Useless Helpful Tidbit 5: The election of 1824 was decided by the House of Representatives after none of the candidates secured a majority of the electoral votes. John Quincy Adams was eventually declared the winner, much to the chagrin of Andrew Jackson, who had won the popular vote.

Useless Helpful Tidbit 6: Campaign tactics can get weird. In the 1964 election, Lyndon B. Johnson's campaign aired the famous "Daisy" ad, which implied that electing Barry Goldwater might lead to nuclear war. It only aired once but left a lasting impact.

Useless Helpful Tidbit 7: The most lopsided presidential election in U.S. history was in 1936, when Franklin D. Roosevelt defeated Alf Landon, winning 523 electoral votes to Landon's 8. Talk about a blowout.

Useless Helpful Tidbit 8: The phrase "October Surprise" refers to a news event deliberately created or timed to influence the outcome of an election, particularly the presidential one. It's the political equivalent of throwing a last-minute Hail Mary pass.

Useless Helpful Tidbit 9: The phrase "October Surprise" refers to a news event deliberately created or timed to influence the outcome of an election, particularly the presidential one. It's the political equivalent of throwing a last-minute Hail Mary pass.

Useless Helpful Tidbit 10: In 1920, following the ratification of the 19th Amendment, women in the United States voted in a presidential election for the first time. Warren G. Harding won in a landslide, possibly with help from newly enfranchised female voters.

Useless Helpful Tidbit 11: The electoral process in the U.S. includes primaries, where parties select their candidates, and caucuses, which are more like town hall meetings where party members debate and decide their candidates.

Useless Helpful Tidbit 12: The "Super Tuesday" concept emerged in the 1980s. Today, many states hold primaries, which can be a make-or-break moment for presidential candidates.

Useless Helpful Tidbit 13: Campaign tactics can get weird. In the 1964 election, Lyndon B. Johnson's campaign aired the famous "Daisy" ad, which implied that electing Barry Goldwater might lead to nuclear war. It only aired once but left a lasting impact.

Useless Helpful Tidbit 14: The Electoral College consists of 538 electors, with a majority of 270 electoral votes required to elect the president. Each state's electors are equal to the number of senators and representatives in Congress.

Useless Helpful Tidbit 15: In 1920, women in the United States voted in a presidential election for the first time following the ratification of the 19th Amendment. Warren G. Harding won in a landslide, possibly with help from newly enfranchised female voters.

Useless Helpful Tidbit 16: Not all U.S. states use a "winner-take-all" approach in the Electoral College. Maine and Nebraska use a proportional system to allocate their electoral votes.

Useless Helpful Tidbit 17: The first televised presidential debates were held in 1960 between John F. Kennedy and Richard Nixon. These debates forever changed the landscape of campaign strategies, highlighting the importance of media presence.

Useless Helpful Tidbit 18: During the 1828 presidential campaign, John Quincy Adams and Andrew Jackson engaged in some of the dirtiest campaigning ever, with accusations ranging from bigamy to pimping. And we thought modern campaigns were rough.

Useless Helpful Tidbit 19: The youngest person ever elected president was John F. Kennedy, who was 43 at the time of his election in 1960. Conversely, the oldest person elected is Joe Biden, who was 78 at his inauguration in 2021.

Useless Helpful Tidbit 20: Grover Cleveland is the only U.S. president to serve two non-consecutive terms, making him the 22nd and 24th president. This unique distinction often puzzles trivia enthusiasts and historians alike.

Great Big Grab Bag of Fun Factoids

Fun Factoid 1: The 1800 election was so contentious that it led to the first peaceful power transfer between political parties in U.S. history, setting a critical precedent for future elections.

Fun Factoid 2: The most expensive election campaign to date was in 2020, with an estimated $14 billion spent on federal elections. It's staggering, considering the presidential salary is $400,000 annually.

Fun Factoid 3: The smallest margin of victory in a U.S. presidential election occurred in 1876 when Rutherford B. Hayes won by just one electoral vote. Every vote truly counts!

Fun Factoid 4: The record for the longest filibuster during a campaign goes to Strom Thurmond, who spoke for 24 hours and 18 minutes against the Civil Rights Act of 1957. While not directly related to the election, it's an impressive (if not tedious) display of endurance.

Fun Factoid 5: The first use of the internet in a presidential campaign was in 1996, with Bob Dole and Bill Clinton's websites. The sites were rudimentary by today's standards but marked the beginning of a new era in digital campaigning.

Chapter 3: Fake News and Media Manipulation

Once upon a time, in the heady days of the 1948 presidential election, the Chicago Tribune famously printed the headline "Dewey Defeats Truman," confident in the polls and the pundits. As it turns out, they were wrong—spectacularly so. The Tribune had jumped the gun, relying on early returns and a series of flawed predictions. President Harry S. Truman, delighted by his unexpected victory, posed for a now-iconic photograph, grinning and holding up the erroneous newspaper for all to see.

The image captured the moment perfectly, highlighting the perils of premature prediction and the delightful unpredictability of American politics. Truman's victory defied nearly all expectations. Pundits, pollsters, and political analysts had primarily written him off, convinced that his opponent, Thomas E. Dewey, was a shoo-in. This miscalculation was partly due to overreliance on early polling data and a failure to gauge the true sentiment of the American electorate.

Truman's campaign strategy played a crucial role in his success. He embarked on a vigorous whistle-stop tour, traveling by train nationwide and delivering speeches directly to the people. His energetic, personable approach resonated with voters who felt overlooked by the Dewey campaign's more aloof and complacent style.

The photograph of Truman holding the "Dewey Defeats Truman" newspaper became one of the most memorable images in American political history. It symbolized the erratic nature of electoral politics and the importance of counting every vote. It reminds us that certainty is elusive in politics and life, and surprises abound. The 1948 election is a classic tale of underdog triumph, illustrating how the human element of campaigning and direct voter engagement can defy even the most confident predictions.

Grab Bag of Useless Helpful Tidbits

1. **The Infamous "Dean Scream":** In 2004, Howard Dean's enthusiastic "Yeah!" during a rally was replayed endlessly, effectively torpedoing his campaign. It was a lesson in how media amplification can turn a momentary lapse into a defining, derailing event.

2. **The Infamous "Dean Scream"**: In 2004, Howard Dean's enthusiastic "Yeah!" during a rally was replayed endlessly, effectively torpedoing his campaign. It was a lesson in how media amplification can turn a momentary lapse into a defining, derailing event.

3. **Social Media Surge**: The 2008 Obama campaign harnessed the power of social media like never before, using platforms like Facebook and Twitter to engage voters, spread messages, and mobilize support. It marked the beginning of a new era in digital political engagement.

4. **The Rise of Fake News**: The term "fake news" gained prominence during the 2016 presidential election, where misinformation and outright falsehoods spread rapidly across social media platforms, influencing public perception and discourse.

5. **The 24-Hour News Cycle**: With the advent of cable news channels like CNN, politics became a constant presence in Americans' lives. This relentless coverage has contributed to heightened political polarization and the sensationalism of political events.

6. **Fact-Checking Frenzy**: In response to the proliferation of fake news, fact-checking websites like Snopes and PolitiFact have become essential tools for discerning truth from fiction in political reporting.

7. **Twitter Tantrums**: President Donald Trump's use of Twitter to communicate directly with the public and bypass traditional media channels was unprecedented. His tweets often made headlines, shaping the news cycle and stirring controversy.

8. **The Power of Memes**: Memes have become a powerful tool in political discourse, capable of distilling complex issues into humorous, shareable content that can go viral and influence public opinion.

9. **The Pundit Problem**: Political pundits on news networks often frame issues that align with their ideological biases, contributing to the echo chamber effect where audiences only hear what they want to believe.

10. **The Benghazi Effect**: The extensive media coverage of the 2012 Benghazi attack highlighted how sustained media focus on a single issue can shape public perception and become a significant political

weapon.

11. **Cable News Bias**: Channels like Fox News and MSNBC are often criticized for their partisan leanings, with Fox being perceived as conservative and MSNBC as liberal, further polarizing the audience.

12. **YouTube's Political Influence**: Politicians and political commentators have leveraged YouTube to reach audiences directly, bypassing traditional media filters and gaining influence among younger viewers.

13. **The Infowars Impact**: Conspiracy theorists like Alex Jones and his Infowars platform have demonstrated how fringe ideas can gain mainstream attention, often blurring the line between fact and fiction.

14. **Deepfake Dilemmas**: Advances in technology have made it possible to create compelling fake videos, known as deepfakes, which pose a significant threat to the integrity of political communication.

15. **Clickbait Campaigns**: Using sensational headlines and misleading content to generate clicks and ad revenue has skewed public perception and prioritized sensationalism over substantive reporting.

16. **Algorithmic Influence**: Social media algorithms prioritize content that generates engagement, often amplifying sensationalist and polarizing material, which can distort the political narrative.

17. **Press Freedom Under Fire**: Politicians criticizing and undermining the press can erode trust in the media and democratic institutions, as seen in various countries where media suppression has become more prevalent.

18. **Late-Night Political Comedy**: Shows like "The Daily Show" and "Last Week Tonight" have blurred the lines between comedy and news, becoming influential political commentary and critique sources.

19. **Media Ownership Concerns**: Consolidating media ownership into a few large corporations has raised concerns about diversity of viewpoints and the potential for media manipulation.

20. **Historic Hoaxes**: Throughout history, numerous political hoaxes and sensationalized stories have captured the public's imagination, from the Great Moon Hoax of 1835 to modern-day conspiracy

theories.

Great Big Grab Bag of Fun Factoids

1. **First Televised Presidential Debate**: The 1960 Kennedy-Nixon debate was the first of its kind, reaching an estimated 70 million viewers and demonstrating television's crucial role in future elections.
2. **Most Tweeted Political Moment**: Barack Obama's 2012 re-election victory tweet, featuring the words "Four more years" and a photo of him hugging Michelle, became the most retweeted message of the time.
3. **Longest Filibuster Covered Life**: 1957, Senator Strom Thurmond's 24-hour filibuster against the Civil Rights Act was extensively covered, setting a record for the longest continuous speech in Senate history.
4. **The "Crossfire" Cancellation**: Jon Stewart's appearance on CNN's "Crossfire" in 2004, where he criticized the show's partisan debate format, was credited with leading to its cancellation, showcasing the power of media critique from comedians.
5. **The "Biden Memes" Phenomenon**: Vice President Joe Biden became an internet sensation with memes depicting him as a lovable, mischievous sidekick to President Obama. These memes illustrated the whimsical side of political media coverage.

Chapter 4: The Legislative Branch

In 1957, Senator Strom Thurmond set the record for the longest filibuster in U.S. history, speaking for an astonishing 24 hours and 18 minutes against the Civil Rights Act. This marathon speech was a test of endurance and a display of a politician's lengths to make a point. Thurmond took steam baths to dehydrate his body and prepare for this epic performance, reducing the need for bathroom breaks. His aides supported him with a peculiar diet of throat lozenges, malted milk tablets, and bits of diced pumpernickel bread to keep his energy and voice going.

Thurmond's speech covered many topics, some relevant, others less so. He famously read from the phone book, recited the Declaration of Independence, and reviewed state election laws, showcasing his determination to speak for as long as possible. This tactic was part of a broader strategy to delay the passage of the Civil Rights Act, a piece of legislation he vehemently opposed.

Despite Thurmond's extraordinary effort, the bill eventually passed, marking a significant moment in the civil rights movement. His filibuster, while ultimately unsuccessful in blocking the legislation, has since become a symbol of the extreme measures lawmakers sometimes employ in pursuit of their political goals. It also highlights the colorful and often absurd nature of political maneuvering in the U.S. Senate. The spectacle of a senator reading from the phone book to avoid yielding the floor illustrates the theatrical aspect of filibusters, making them memorable events in legislative history. Thurmond's record remains a testament to American politics' unique and sometimes bizarre traditions.

Grab Bag of Useless Helpful Tidbits

1. **The Camel Corps:** In the 1850s, the U.S. Army experimented with using camels for transportation in the southwestern United States. Congress approved the funding, but the project was eventually abandoned as the camels proved challenging to manage.
2. **Congressional Brawls:** The most infamous congressional brawl occurred in 1856 when Representative Preston Brooks beat Senator Charles Sumner with a cane on the Senate floor, nearly killing him, over a speech Sumner had given criticizing slaveholders.
3. **Peculiar Proposals**: In 1893, Representative Lucas Miller of Wisconsin proposed a bill to abolish the Army and Navy and replace them with a standing committee of one person to adjudicate all international disputes.
4. **The "Famous Fistfight"**: In 1798, Congressmen Matthew Lyon and Roger Griswold engaged in a physical altercation on the House floor, complete with canes and tongs, during a heated debate over the Sedition Act.
5. **The "Cornhusker Kickback"**: A deal made during the negotiations for the Affordable Care Act in 2009, where Nebraska Senator Ben

Nelson secured extra Medicaid funding for his state in exchange for his crucial vote.

6. **The "Bridge to Nowhere"**: A proposed bridge in Alaska, which became a symbol of government waste and pork-barrel spending, highlighting the often questionable allocation of federal funds.

7. **Longest Serving Member**: Senator Robert Byrd of West Virginia is the longest-serving member of Congress, having served for over 57 years.

8. **Youngest Member Ever**: William Charles Cole Claiborne was elected to Congress at 22 in 1797 before the minimum age requirement of 25 was enforced.

9. **Oldest Member Ever**: Strom Thurmond was the oldest member of Congress. He served until he was 100 and retired in 2003.

10. **The "Gag Rule"**: From 1836 to 1844, Congress passed a series prohibiting the discussion of abolitionist petitions, demonstrating the contentious nature of slavery debates even before the Civil War.

11. **The "Do Nothing Congress"**: The 80th Congress (1947-1948) earned this nickname from President Harry Truman for its lack of legislative productivity, passing only a fraction of proposed bills.

12. **The Great Senate Cotillion**: In 1946, newly elected Senator Glen H. Taylor arrived at the Senate in a cowboy outfit, complete with a ten-gallon hat, boots, and fringed shirt, causing quite a stir among his colleagues.

13. **The "Kettle of Fish"**: In 1833, Senator John Randolph of Roanoke insulted the entire Senate by referring to it as "this wretched hive of scum and villainy," borrowing a line centuries before Star Wars would make it famous.

14. **The Senate Candy Desk**: Since 1968, a desk near the entrance of the Senate has been stocked with candy, originally by Senator George Murphy and continued by subsequent Senators, to provide sweet treats to colleagues.

15. **The "Cucumber King"**: In the 1800s, Representative Charles Sumner successfully argued for including cucumbers as a tax-exempt agricultural product, earning him the quirky nickname.

16. **The "Friday Night Massacre"**: In 1973, during the Watergate

scandal, President Nixon ordered the firing of special prosecutor Archibald Cox, leading to the resignations of the Attorney General and Deputy Attorney General.

17. **Strange Speeches**: In 1954, Senator William Proxmire delivered a speech listing the Senate's most wasteful spending items, including a study on why people fall in love, kicking off his famous "Golden Fleece Awards."

18. **Senate Bean Soup**: Since 1903, the Senate dining hall has served bean soup daily, regardless of the season, following a tradition started by Senator Fred Dubois of Idaho.

19. **The "Sleeping Senator"**: Senator Robert Byrd was known for napping during Senate sessions, often wrapping himself in a blanket at his desk.

20. **The "Pig Book"**: Published annually by Citizens Against Government Waste, the "Pig Book" highlights the most egregious examples of pork-barrel spending and keeps a humorous yet critical eye on congressional appropriations.

Great Big Grab Bag of Fun Factoids

1. **The Youngest Member Ever Elected**: William Charles Cole Claiborne holds the record, was elected at age 22, and was three years younger than the constitutional requirement.

2. **The Oldest Member Ever to Serve**: Strom Thurmond holds the title. He served until he was 100, and his Senate career spanned nearly five decades.

3. **First Woman in Congress**: Jeannette Rankin of Montana, elected in 1916, was the first woman to serve in the U.S. Congress four years before women had the right to vote nationwide.

4. **The Shortest Congressional Term**: Effingham Lawrence holds the record for the shortest term in Congress, serving just one day in 1875 as a Representative from Louisiana.

5. **Record for Voting**: Senator William Proxmire holds the record for the most consecutive votes in the Senate, casting 10,252 consecutive votes over 22 years without ever missing one.

Chapter 5: The Executive Branch

In 1923, President Calvin Coolidge received an unusual gift—a live raccoon intended for the White House Thanksgiving dinner. Coolidge, however, decided the raccoon was too cute to eat. Instead, he named her Rebecca and made her a household pet, often seen walking around the White House on a leash. Rebecca quickly became a beloved member of the Coolidge family, even receiving a collar engraved with "White House Raccoon."

Rebecca's arrival at the White House was met with surprise and delight. She was a spirited addition to the Coolidge menagerie, which already included dogs, birds, and even a pygmy hippo named Billy. Rebecca was known for her playful antics, including mischievously untying shoelaces and exploring the nooks and crannies of the presidential residence.

The raccoon's presence also served a diplomatic purpose. When foreign dignitaries visited, they were often charmed by Rebecca's unique character, providing a memorable and endearing aspect to their visit. Her popularity was such that she even had her press coverage, with newspapers across the country publishing stories about her latest adventures.

Coolidge's affection for Rebecca indicated his overall love for animals, which endeared him to the American public. Despite his reputation for being quiet and reserved, the president's playful interactions with his pets showed a different, more personable side. Rebecca's legacy continued even after Coolidge left office, symbolizing the unexpected joys and lighter moments that can punctuate the serious business of governing a nation.

Grab Bag of Useless Helpful Tidbits

1. **Presidential Pets**: From George Washington's hunting dogs to Barack Obama's Portuguese Water Dogs, presidential pets have ranged from the ordinary to the exotic, including John Quincy Adams' pet alligator.
2. **Teddy Roosevelt's Menagerie**: Theodore Roosevelt's White House was practically a zoo, with animals like a lion, a zebra, a hyena, and even a bear, reflecting his love for wildlife and adventure.

3. **Executive Orders**: Franklin D. Roosevelt issued the most executive orders of any president, totaling 3,728 during his four terms, demonstrating the extensive use of executive power.

4. **Eccentric Habits**: John Quincy Adams was known for his habit of skinny-dipping in the Potomac River every morning. This activity led to an exciting encounter with a female journalist who requested an interview while he was in the water.

5. **Lincoln's Cats**: Abraham Lincoln loved cats and often brought strays into the White House. His fondness for felines was so well-known that he once remarked, "Dixie is smarter than my whole cabinet!"

6. **Odd Executive Orders**: 1984 Ronald Reagan issued an executive order designating July as National Ice Cream Month, reflecting his fondness for the frozen treat.

7. **Oval Office Decor**: Presidents often personalize the Oval Office with unique items; for example, Lyndon B. Johnson had a Fresnel lens from a lighthouse, symbolizing his guiding role as president.

8. **Silent Cal's Pranks**: Calvin Coolidge, known for his quiet demeanor, had a naughty side. Once, he pressed all the White House call buttons and hid to see the staff's frantic response.

9. **Presidential Ghosts**: The White House is reputedly haunted by the ghost of Abraham Lincoln, reportedly seen by numerous presidents and their guests, adding a spooky layer to the executive mansion.

10. **Personal Beliefs and Policies**: Jimmy Carter, a devout Christian, often incorporated his faith into his policies, such as emphasizing human rights in foreign policy decisions.

11. **Presidential Hoaxes**: 1835 President Andrew Jackson fell victim to the Great Moon Hoax, a widely circulated story claiming that life had been discovered on the moon.

12. **Harry Truman's Piano**: President Truman loved playing the piano and even gave an impromptu performance at the White House for a visiting delegation of governors.

13. **FDR's Fireside Chats**: Franklin D. Roosevelt used his Fireside Chats to communicate directly with the American people, revolutionizing presidential communication in the radio era.

14. **Carter's UFO Sighting**: Before becoming president, Jimmy Carter

claimed to have seen a UFO in 1969, a story that added to his reputation as a president who believed in transparency and truth.

15. **Presidential Fitness**: Theodore Roosevelt was known for his vigorous fitness regime, which included boxing, jiu-jitsu, and hikes through Rock Creek Park in Washington, D.C.

16. **Kennedy's Rocking Chair**: John F. Kennedy's use of a rocking chair for back pain relief became iconic, symbolizing his youthful yet frail health.

17. **Bush's Pretzel Incident**: 2002 President George W. Bush fainted after choking on a pretzel while watching a football game, which brought some fun to his tenure.

18. **Nixon's Bowling Alley**: Richard Nixon installed a one-lane bowling alley in the White House basement, reflecting his love for the sport and desire for a stress-relief outlet.

19. **Obama's Beer Summit**: 2009 President Obama hosted a "Beer Summit" to resolve a racially charged incident, showing a modern president's approach to addressing sensitive social issues.

20. **Jefferson's Mammoth Cheese**: A group of Baptists from Massachusetts gifted Thomas Jefferson a 1,235-pound block of cheese, known as the "Mammoth Cheese," which he proudly displayed in the White House.

Great Big Grab Bag of Fun Factoids

1. **Shortest Inaugural Speech**: George Washington holds the record for the shortest inaugural address, consisting of just 135 words, delivered during his second inauguration in 1793.

2. **Longest Inaugural Speech**: William Henry Harrison delivered the most extended inaugural address, at over 8,000 words, in 1841. The lengthy speech in cold weather contributed to his death from pneumonia just a month later.

3. **First Televised Inauguration**: Harry S. Truman's 1949 inauguration was the first to be televised, bringing the ceremony to millions of Americans and setting a new standard for presidential visibility.

4. **Youngest President**: Theodore Roosevelt was the youngest to assume

the presidency at 42, following the assassination of William McKinley. His vigor and energy in the office were evident.

5. **Oldest President**: Joe Biden became the oldest president to assume office, inaugurating at 78 in 2021. This highlights the evolving demographics and expectations of presidential candidates.

Chapter 6: The Judicial Branch

In 1928, the Supreme Court heard a case that revolved around a seemingly trivial issue: Henry T. Rainey sued the government for damages caused by an escaped goat. The case, known as United States v. Rainey, arose when Rainey's goat, which he claimed was a prized breeder, wandered onto government property and was accidentally killed by federal workers. Rainey sought compensation, arguing that the government had been negligent.

The Supreme Court, faced with this peculiar matter, had to determine whether the government was liable for the loss of Rainey's goat. In a decision that balanced legal principles with a touch of humor, the Court ruled against Rainey, stating that the government could not be held responsible for the actions of an animal that had roamed freely onto its property. This quirky case highlights the occasionally bizarre nature of the issues that reach the highest court in the land and serves as a reminder that the Supreme Court's docket can sometimes be filled with the most unexpected of disputes.

Grab Bag of Useless Helpful Tidbits

1. **The Midnight Appointments**: In 1801, outgoing President John Adams appointed several Federalist judges at the last minute, leading to the famous Marbury v. Madison case, which established judicial review.
2. **The Court's Oddest Case**: In 1893, Nix v. Hedden ruled that tomatoes are legally vegetables, not fruits, based on their use in meals, despite their botanical classification.
3. **Justice's Quirks**: Justice Hugo Black, known for his dedication, often worked so late that he slept in his chambers to maximize productivity.

4. **Landmark Decisions**: Brown v. Board of Education (1954) declared racial segregation in public schools unconstitutional, dramatically altering American society.

5. **Unexpected Consequences**: The Dred Scott decision (1857) intended to settle the issue of slavery but instead inflamed tensions, hastening the onset of the Civil War.

6. **The Longest Filibuster for a Nominee**: Abe Fortas faced a 75-day filibuster over his nomination as Chief Justice in 1968, which ultimately led to his withdrawal.

7. **Political Battles**: Bush v. Gore (2000) effectively decided the presidential election, illustrating the Supreme Court's significant influence on political outcomes.

8. **The Court's First Woman**: Sandra Day O'Connor, appointed in 1981, became the first female justice, breaking a significant gender barrier in the judiciary.

9. **Justice Scalia's Wit**: Antonin Scalia was known for his sharp wit, and his humorous and intelligent questions often livened up oral arguments.

10. **Judicial Impeachment**: Justice Samuel Chase was impeached in 1804 for alleged political bias but was acquitted by the Senate, reinforcing judicial independence.

11. **The "Switch in Time"**: 1937 Justice Owen Roberts switched his vote on New Deal legislation, preventing a court-packing plan and maintaining the Court's structure.

12. **Supreme Court Ghosts**: The Supreme Court building is rumored to be haunted by the ghost of Justice Joseph Story, who allegedly roams the halls.

13. **Longest Serving Justice**: William O. Douglas served on the Court for over 36 years, from 1939 to 1975, making him the longest-serving justice in history.

14. **The Court's Own Gym**: The Supreme Court building includes a gymnasium with a basketball court, humorously dubbed "the highest court in the land."

15. **Unique Petitions**: The Court has received bizarre petitions, including one from a man seeking to trademark the word "heebie-

jeebies."

16. **Judicial Review**: Established in Marbury v. Madison (1803), this principle allows the Court to strike down laws it deems unconstitutional, a cornerstone of American law.

17. **The Katzenjammer Kids Case**: In 1911, the Court ruled on a comic strip copyright case, highlighting its role in protecting intellectual property.

18. **The Most Senior Justice**: The most senior associate justice gets to choose their office and is privileged to speak first in private conferences.

19. **Original Jurisdiction**: The Supreme Court has original jurisdiction in cases involving ambassadors and state disputes, a rare but critical aspect of its role.

20. **Justice Ginsburg's Workouts**: Ruth Bader Ginsburg became famous for her rigorous workout routine, which she maintained well into her eighties, inspiring many.

Great Big Grab Bag of Fun Factoids

1. **Longest-Serving Justices**: William O. Douglas served 36 years, while John Paul Stevens served for 35 years, making them the longest-serving justices in Supreme Court history.

2. **Most Controversial Nomination**: Robert Bork's 1987 nomination was rejected after a highly contentious confirmation process, leading to the term "borked" for failed nominations.

3. **First Televised Hearing**: The Supreme Court's proceedings are not televised, but the confirmation hearings for nominees are, with the first televised hearing occurring for Clarence Thomas in 1991.

4. **Oldest Appointee**: Horace Lurton, appointed at age 65 in 1909, was the oldest person ever appointed to the Supreme Court.

5. **Youngest Justice**: Joseph Story, appointed at age 32 in 1811, remains the youngest person ever to serve on the Supreme Court.

Chapter 7: State and Local Politics

In 1938, a small town in Indiana became the epicenter of one of the most amusing—and slightly embarrassing—episodes in local politics. The city of Whiting, known for its annual Pierogi Festival today, decided to elect a "Goat Mayor." The election was part of a fundraising campaign for the local fire department, with the candidates being various goats from local farms. The town's citizens enthusiastically took to the idea, casting their votes for their favorite goat.

The winning goat, named "Billy," was inaugurated in a festive ceremony with a tiny mayoral sash. Billy's "tenure" was filled with playful antics, such as nibbling on official documents and bleating loudly during town meetings. His reign as Goat Mayor was a light-hearted distraction and a surprisingly effective fundraiser, bringing the community together and raising significant funds for the fire department.

The Goat Mayor incident highlights the quirky charm of small-town politics, where the community spirit and a good sense of humor can turn a simple fundraiser into a memorable event. It reminds us that not all politics are serious business; sometimes, a little fun is exactly what a town needs.

Grab Bag of Useless Helpful Tidbits

1. **Odd State Laws**: In Arizona, it's illegal for a donkey to sleep in a bathtub. This law was enacted after a flood in the 1920s displaced a donkey in a tub, causing chaos.

2. **Unique Government Structures**: New England towns often hold town meetings, a form of direct democratic rule in which citizens vote on local issues directly.

3. **The Great Emu War**: In 1932, Western Australia faced an "invasion" of emus. The government sent soldiers to curb the population, but the emus proved surprisingly elusive, and the event is remembered as a humorous failure.

4. **Notable State Scandals**: The 2008 scandal involving Illinois Governor Rod Blagojevich, who tried to sell President-elect Barack Obama's vacated Senate seat, stands out in state political history.

5. **Voting Rights**: Debates over voter ID laws, such as those in Texas

and Georgia, highlight ongoing tensions over voter registration and access to the polls.

6. **Citizen Rights**: Some states allow non-citizens to vote in local elections. For example, in certain cities in Maryland, legal immigrants can vote in municipal elections.

7. **Illegal Aliens and Rights**: California has been at the forefront of granting rights to undocumented immigrants, such as allowing them to obtain driver's licenses.

8. **State Constitutions**: The Alabama state constitution, with over 800 amendments, is the longest in the world, demonstrating the complexity of state governance.

9. **Local Ordinances**: In Quitman, Georgia, chickens are prohibited from crossing the road, a humorous but honest example of quirky local laws.

10. **Political Dynasties**: Some states, like Massachusetts with the Kennedy family, have notable political dynasties that influence local and national politics.

11. **Recall Elections**: California's gubernatorial recall process is famous, notably when Arnold Schwarzenegger replaced Gray Davis in 2003.

12. **The "Lizard Man"**: In 1988, South Carolina reported seeing a creature called the "Lizard Man," which local politicians used to boost tourism and the regional economy.

13. **The "New York Soda Ban"**: New York City attempted to ban large sugary drinks in 2012, a controversial move that sparked significant public debate and legal battles.

14. **Quirky Campaign Promises**: In 1991, a cat named Stubbs was elected mayor of Talkeetna, Alaska, serving in a primarily ceremonial role until 2017.

1. **State Symbols**: Texas takes state pride seriously, with official state symbols including the longhorn, the bluebonnet, and even the state pepper, the jalapeño.

2. **"Pennsylvania's Tunnels"**: Pittsburgh has an extensive network of abandoned tunnels and mines, occasionally used as political talking points in local campaigns.

3. **The "Big Dig"**: Boston's Central Artery/Tunnel Project, known as the Big Dig, was one of the most complex and expensive highway projects in U.S. history, highlighting issues of urban planning and state funding.
4. **State Holidays**: Some states have unique holidays, like Alaska's Seward's Day, celebrating the purchase of Alaska from Russia.
5. **Interstate Compacts**: States often enter into agreements with each other to manage shared resources, like the Colorado River Compact, which allocates water rights among seven states.
6. **Legal Oddities**: In Kentucky, carrying ice cream in your back pocket is illegal, a law initially intended to prevent horse theft.

Great Big Grab Bag of Fun Factoids

1. **Oldest State Constitution**: Massachusetts has the oldest functioning written constitution, drafted in 1780 by John Adams and still in use today.
2. **Bizarre Local Ordinances**: In Boulder, Colorado, it is illegal to roll a boulder down a hill, a humorous but factual ordinance reflecting the town's mountainous terrain.
3. **Most Amendments**: Alabama's state constitution has been amended over 900 times, making it the most amended constitution in the world.
4. **Shortest State Constitution**: Vermont's state constitution is one of the shortest, reflecting the state's preference for simplicity and clarity in its governance documents.
5. **Unique Local Officials**: Rabbit Hash, Kentucky's mayoral elections are unique. The town has elected a dog as mayor multiple times, highlighting its quirky sense of community and humor.

Chapter 8: Political Parties and Movements

In 1968, the United States witnessed one of its most unusual and humorous presidential campaigns. The Youth International Party, better known as the

Yippies, nominated a pig named Pigasus for President. The Yippies, a countercultural movement, staged this as a protest against the political establishment and the Vietnam War. The nominating event occurred in Chicago, where the pig was presented to the media and a crowd of supporters.

The police quickly intervened, arresting Pigasus and several Yippie leaders. The image of law enforcement detaining a pig captured the absurdity and theatrical nature of the protest, drawing significant media attention. Though not intended as a serious political movement, the Yippies' antics highlighted the growing discontent and desire for change among the younger generation. Pigasus' campaign is remembered as a humorous yet pointed critique of the political system, underscoring the lengths activists will go to make their voices heard.

Grab Bag of Useless Helpful Tidbits

1. **The Rise of the Whigs**: The Whig Party, active in the mid-19th century, emerged in opposition to Andrew Jackson's policies and played a significant role in American politics before dissolving in the 1850s.
2. **Defunct Parties**: The Know-Nothing Party, officially the American Party, was an anti-immigrant and anti-Catholic movement in the 1850s that quickly faded after its peak.
3. **The Bull Moose Party**: Formed by Theodore Roosevelt in 1912 after a split in the Republican Party, the Progressive Party, also known as the Bull Moose Party, emphasized progressive reforms but dissolved shortly after.
4. **The Prohibition Party**: Founded in 1869, it advocated for alcohol prohibition and remains the oldest third party in the U.S., though its influence has waned significantly.
5. **Socialist Movements**: The Socialist Party of America, established in 1901, peaked in the early 20th century. Eugene V. Debs was its prominent leader, advocating for workers' rights and social reforms.
6. **The Green Party**: Established in the 1980s, it focuses on environmental issues, social justice, and grassroots democracy, though it struggles to gain major electoral success.
7. **The Libertarian Party**: Founded in 1971, it advocates for minimal

government intervention in personal and economic matters, often attracting voters disillusioned with the two major parties.

8. **The Populist Party**: The People's Party emerged in the 1890s, advocating for the interests of farmers and laborers. It had notable influence before merging with the Democrats.

9. **The Tea Party Movement**: Beginning in 2009, the Tea Party was a conservative movement within the Republican Party that advocated for reducing government spending and taxes.

10. **The Occupy Movement**: Starting in 2011 with Occupy Wall Street, this movement protested against economic inequality and the influence of corporations in politics.

11. **The Dixiecrats**: A segregationist states' rights party formed in 1948 by Southern Democrats who opposed the civil rights platforms of the National Democratic Party.

12. **The Free Soil Party**: Active in the 1840s and 1850s, it opposed expanding slavery into the western territories and eventually merged with the Republican Party.

13. **The Silent Majority**: A term popularized by President Nixon, referring to the perceived majority of Americans who did not publicly protest but supported his policies.

14. **The Black Panther Party**: Founded in 1966, the Black Panther Party advocated for African American rights and self-defense and symbolized militant civil rights activism.

1. **State Symbols**: Texas takes state pride seriously, with official state symbols including the longhorn, the bluebonnet, and even the state pepper, the jalapeño.

2. **"Pennsylvania's Tunnels"**: Pittsburgh has an extensive network of abandoned tunnels and mines, occasionally used as political talking points in local campaigns.

3. **The "Big Dig"**: Boston's Central Artery/Tunnel Project, known as the Big Dig, was one of the most complex and expensive highway projects in U.S. history, highlighting issues of urban planning and state funding.

4. **State Holidays**: Some states have unique holidays, like Alaska's

Seward's Day, celebrating the purchase of Alaska from Russia.

5. **Interstate Compacts**: States often enter into agreements with each other to manage shared resources, like the Colorado River Compact, which allocates water rights among seven states.

6. **Legal Oddities**: In Kentucky, carrying ice cream in your back pocket is illegal, a law initially intended to prevent horse theft.

Great Big Grab Bag of Fun Factoids

1. **Oldest State Constitution**: Massachusetts has the oldest functioning written constitution, drafted in 1780 by John Adams and still in use today.

2. **Bizarre Local Ordinances**: In Boulder, Colorado, it is illegal to roll a boulder down a hill, a humorous but factual ordinance reflecting the town's mountainous terrain.

3. **Most Amendments**: Alabama's state constitution has been amended over 900 times, making it the most amended constitution in the world.

4. **Shortest State Constitution**: Vermont's state constitution is one of the shortest, reflecting the state's preference for simplicity and clarity in its governance documents.

5. **Unique Local Officials**: Rabbit Hash, Kentucky's mayoral elections are unique. The town has elected a dog as mayor multiple times, highlighting its quirky sense of community and humor.

Chapter 9: Political Scandals

In 1933, one of the quirkiest political scandals involved the infamous "Kidnapping of the Lindbergh Baby." The case gripped the nation as the 20-month-old son of famed aviator Charles Lindbergh was abducted from the family home. The crime was a sad event that captivated the media and the public. However, a humorous twist occurred when President Franklin D. Roosevelt was dragged into the fray by a bizarre request.

Convinced that the famed crime-solving cartoon character Dick Tracy could help solve the case, a desperate citizen wrote to Roosevelt, urging him to recruit the fictional detective. The citizen's plea was heartfelt, showing just how famous and trusted Dick Tracy was in the eyes of the public. While Roosevelt obviously couldn't summon a comic strip hero to assist, he responded with a good-natured letter, acknowledging the citizen's enthusiasm and expressing his hope for a swift resolution to the case.

This amusing episode highlighted how deeply entrenched popular culture was in the public's consciousness, even during severe national events. It also showcased Roosevelt's ability to maintain a sense of humor and personally connect with citizens despite his responsibilities' gravity. The president's light-hearted reply humanized him, showing that he could engage with the concerns of ordinary Americans, even if those concerns were a bit outlandish. This story is a testament to the unique intersection of pop culture and politics and how leaders can use humor to bridge the gap between their office and the public.

Grab Bag of Useless Helpful Tidbits

1. **The Teapot Dome Scandal**: In the 1920s, Secretary of the Interior Albert B. Fall leased Navy petroleum reserves at Teapot Dome, Wyoming, to private oil companies in exchange for bribes, leading to his imprisonment.
2. **Watergate**: The 1972 break-in at the Democratic National Committee headquarters led to President Nixon's resignation in 1974, highlighting the abuse of power and subsequent cover-up by the Nixon administration.
3. **The Iran-Contra Affair**: During the 1980s, senior Reagan administration officials secretly facilitated the sale of arms to Iran, which was under an arms embargo, and used the proceeds to fund Contra rebels in Nicaragua.
4. **The Lewinsky Scandal**: President Bill Clinton's affair with White House intern Monica Lewinsky led to his impeachment by the House in 1998, though the Senate acquitted him.
5. **The Credit Mobilier Scandal**: In the 1870s, Union Pacific Railroad executives formed the Credit Mobilier construction company and

used it to fraudulently skim off railroad profits, bribing several members of Congress in the process.

6. **The Whiskey Ring**: In the 1870s, government officials and whiskey distillers conspired to defraud the government of tax revenues, leading to indictments and convictions, including President Grant's private secretary.

7. **The Keating Five**: In 1989, five U.S. Senators were accused of intervening for Charles Keating, whose savings and loan association collapsed, costing taxpayers billions.

8. **The Enron Scandal**: In 2001, the energy company Enron collapsed due to massive accounting fraud, leading to the imprisonment of several executives and widespread financial fallout.

9. **The Jack Abramoff Scandal**: Lobbyist Jack Abramoff was found guilty in 2006 of fraud, tax evasion, and conspiracy to bribe public officials, highlighting the corruption in lobbying practices.

10. **The Blagojevich Scandal**: In 2008, Illinois Governor Rod Blagojevich was arrested for attempting to sell President Obama's vacated Senate seat, which led to his impeachment and removal from office.

11. **The Pentagon Papers**: In 1971, Daniel Ellsberg leaked a classified report on U.S. involvement in Vietnam, revealing government deception and fueling public opposition to the war.

12. **The Whitewater Controversy**: A real estate investment involving Bill and Hillary Clinton became the subject of multiple investigations in the 1990s, though the Clintons were never charged with wrongdoing.

13. **The Plame Affair**: In 2003, the identity of CIA operative Valerie Plame was leaked, leading to the conviction of Vice President Cheney's chief of staff, Scooter Libby, for perjury and obstruction of justice.

14. **The Teapot Dome Scandal's Legacy**: This scandal led to significant reforms in U.S. government oversight and ethics laws, including establishing the Senate Committee on Public Lands.

15. **The Bridgegate Scandal:** In 2013, aides to New Jersey Governor Chris Christie orchestrated traffic jams on the George Washington

Bridge to punish a political opponent, leading to convictions for several officials.

16. **The ABSCAM Sting**: In the late 1970s, the FBI set up a sting operation that led to the conviction of several members of Congress for

17. **The Gilded Age Scandals:** This period was rife with political corruption, including the Tammany Hall political machine and the graft and bribery schemes of "Boss" Tweed in New York City.

18. **The Hamilton-Burr Duel**: Vice President Aaron Burr fatally shot Alexander Hamilton in a duel in 1804, ending Burr's political career and casting a shadow over early American politics.

19. **The Chappaquiddick Incident**: In 1969, Senator Ted Kennedy drove off a bridge, resulting in the death of passenger Mary Jo Kopechne, which severely damaged his political aspirations.

20. **The Travelgate Controversy:** Early in the Clinton administration, the firing of White House Travel Office employees led to allegations of cronyism and misuse of FBI files.

Great Big Grab Bag of Fun Factoids

1. **Most Expensive Investigation**: The investigation into the Enron scandal cost an estimated $40 million, making it one of the most expensive corporate fraud investigations in history.

2. **Strangest Accusations**: In 1868, President Andrew Johnson was impeached partly for firing his Secretary of War, Edwin Stanton, in violation of the Tenure of Office Act, leading to his narrow acquittal by one vote.

3. **Longest Senate Filibuster**: Strom Thurmond's filibuster against the Civil Rights Act of 1957 lasted 24 hours and 18 minutes, the longest single-person filibuster in Senate history.

4. **First Presidential Resignation**: On August 8, 1974, Richard Nixon became the first and only U.S. president to resign amid the Watergate scandal.

5. **Most Investigated President**: Bill Clinton faced numerous investigations, including Whitewater, Travelgate, Filegate, and the

Lewinsky scandal, which led to his impeachment in 1998, though the Senate acquitted him.

Chapter 10: Voter Rights and Regulations

In 1844, New York City hosted one of the most chaotic elections in American history, dubbed the "Election of the Dead Rabbits." No, this wasn't a furry uprising. The Dead Rabbits were an infamous Irish gang who decided to sway the vote by any means necessary, including brawling in the streets. The city's polling places were more like wrestling rings as rival gangs, including the Bowery Boys, clashed violently. Voters were coerced, ballots were stolen, and some people were so "enthusiastic" they voted multiple times under different names. One man allegedly cast 22 votes! This chaotic scene was a poignant (and somewhat ridiculous) reminder of the importance of voter integrity and led to significant electoral reforms. Fast forward to today, and while the brawls have largely subsided, the fight for fair voting rights continues in a much less physically violent—but no less contentious—arena.

Grab Bag of Useless Helpful Tidbits

1. **Historical Struggles**: The 15th Amendment, ratified in 1870, granted African American men the right to vote, but it took nearly a century and the Civil Rights Movement to break down barriers like literacy tests and poll taxes.
2. **Women's Suffrage**: The 19th Amendment, passed in 1920, finally granted women the right to vote, thanks to tireless advocacy by suffragettes like Susan B. Anthony and Elizabeth Cady Stanton.
3. **Youth Vote**: The 26th Amendment, ratified in 1971, lowered the voting age from 21 to 18, mainly in response to arguments that those old enough to be drafted for war should also have a say in electing their leaders.
4. **Voter ID Laws**: As of 2021, 36 states have some form of voter ID requirement. These laws are controversial, with supporters arguing they prevent fraud and critics claiming they disenfranchise minorities

and low-income voters.

5. **Early Voting**: In the 2020 presidential election, nearly 100 million Americans took advantage of early voting, whether by mail or in person, a record high driven by the COVID-19 pandemic.

6. **Absentee Ballots**: Absentee voting started during the Civil War to allow soldiers to vote from the battlefield. Today, it's a vital option for those who can't attend the polls on Election Day.

7. **Voter Turnout**: The highest voter turnout in U.S. history was in the 2020 election, with 66.8% of eligible voters casting ballots.

8. **Felony Disenfranchisement**: Over 6 million Americans could not vote in 2020 due to felony convictions. Some states have stringent laws, while others, like Maine and Vermont, allow inmates to vote from prison.

9. **Motor Voter Act**: Enacted in 1993, this law made voter registration easier by allowing people to register when they get their driver's license.

10. **Help America Vote Act**: Passed in 2002, this act aimed to reform voting processes and address issues from the 2000 presidential election, including upgrading voting equipment.

11. **Electoral College**: Established by the Constitution, the Electoral College is a unique system in which electors, rather than a direct popular vote, ultimately elect the president.

12. **Gerrymandering**: This practice involves drawing electoral district boundaries to favor one party over another and remains a contentious issue in American politics.

13. **Voting Rights Act of 1965**: This landmark legislation prohibited racial discrimination in voting and significantly increased voter registration and participation among minorities.

14. **Native American Voting Rights**: Native Americans were not granted U.S. citizenship and the right to vote until 1924, and many states didn't fully comply until the 1960s.

15. **Provisional Ballots**: These are used when eligibility is questioned. The voter can cast a ballot set aside until eligibility is confirmed.

16. **Same-Day Registration**: 21 states and the District of Columbia allow voters to register on Election Day, which studies show increases

voter turnout.

17. **Electronic Voting Machines**: Introduced in the 1960s, these machines have evolved but remain controversial due to concerns about hacking and reliability.

18. **International Voting**: U.S. citizens living abroad can vote by absentee ballot, a practice supported by the Uniformed and Overseas Citizens Absentee Voting Act.

19. **Early Voting**: By 2020, 43 states and the District of Columbia offered some form of early voting, allowing voters more flexibility.

20. **Voter Purges**: States periodically remove inactive or ineligible voters from their rolls, a practice that can prevent fraud but also risks disenfranchising eligible voters.

Great Big Grab Bag of Fun Factoids

1. **Most Restrictive State**: Georgia is often cited for its stringent voter ID laws and controversial voter roll purges.

2. **Most Lenient State**: Oregon, which conducts all elections by mail, boasts one of the highest voter participation rates in the country.

3. **First to Vote**: In 1893, New Zealand became the first self-governing country to grant women the right to vote.

4. **Voting Age**: Brazil has one of the most inclusive voting systems, where voting is mandatory for citizens aged 18-70 and optional for those aged 16-17 and over 70.

5. **Highest Turnout**: Belgium often has the highest voter turnout in the world, thanks to compulsory voting laws.

These tidbits and factoids are designed to inform, amuse, and maybe even spark a lively debate about the intricate dance of democracy and the ongoing quest for fair and accessible voting rights.

Chapter 11: Political Deal-Making

In the early 1800s, the U.S. Senate was known for its colorful characters, but none more so than Senator Thomas Hart Benton of Missouri. Benton was a fierce advocate for Western expansion, and his fiery temper was legendary.

During one particularly heated debate over land policy, Benton was at odds with fellow Senator Henry Clay of Kentucky. Known as the "Great Compromiser," Clay attempted to smooth things with a well-timed joke, but Benton didn't have it. He leaped from his seat, roaring that he would "soil his hands on no man's filthy face!" In response, Clay, always the statesman, quipped, "Then perhaps you'll settle for my clean one."

The chamber erupted in laughter, and while the two men never quite saw eye to eye, the incident underscored the peculiar mix of humor, bravado, and strategic maneuvering that often defines political deal-making. Like so many from the annals of political history, this story reminds us that sometimes a good laugh is just as crucial as a good policy.

Grab Bag of Useless Helpful Tidbits

1. **The Missouri Compromise (1820)**: This agreement allowed Missouri to enter the Union as a slave state and Maine as a free state, maintaining the balance of power between North and South.
2. **Compromise of 1850**: Five bills to defuse tensions between slave and free states following the Mexican-American War. It included the controversial Fugitive Slave Act.
3. **The Great Compromise (1787)**: The Connecticut Compromise established the bicameral legislature of the U.S. Congress, balancing representation for both large and small states.
4. **The Corrupt Bargain (1824)**: Allegations arose that Henry Clay helped John Quincy Adams win the presidency in exchange for being appointed Secretary of State, tarnishing both men's reputations.
5. **Teapot Dome Scandal (1920s)**: A notorious example of back-room deals and corruption, where government officials leased Navy petroleum reserves to private oil companies for bribes.
6. **Louisiana Purchase (1803)**: President Thomas Jefferson's purchase of Louisiana from France, a deal that doubled the size of the U.S. and

involved intense behind-the-scenes negotiations.

7. **Camp David Accords (1978)**: President Jimmy Carter brokered this historic peace agreement between Egypt and Israel, demonstrating the power of diplomatic deal-making.

8. **Kansas-Nebraska Act (1854)**: This allowed territories to decide about slavery, leading to violent conflicts known as "Bleeding Kansas."

9. **Senate Filibuster Deals**: Filibusters have often been used as leverage in political deal-making, with senators negotiating deals to end lengthy speeches and procedural delays.

10. **The New Deal (1930s)**: Franklin D. Roosevelt's series of programs and reforms to combat the Great Depression involved numerous compromises with Congress.

11. **The Gadsden Purchase (1853)**: The U.S. bought land from Mexico to facilitate the building of a southern transcontinental railroad, exemplifying strategic deal-making.

12. **Medicare and Medicaid (1965)**: Part of President Lyndon B. Johnson's Great Society, these programs were established after extensive legislative negotiations and compromises.

13. **The Iran-Contra Affair (1980s)**: A clandestine deal where the Reagan administration secretly facilitated arms sales to Iran, using the proceeds to fund Contra rebels in Nicaragua.

14. **Paris Climate Agreement (2015)**: This international climate change treaty involves intricate negotiations and compromises between nearly 200 countries.

15. **The 3/5 Compromise (1787)**: This was a profoundly contentious agreement during the Constitutional Convention, in which enslaved people were counted as three-fifths of a person for representation and taxation.

16. **Cuban Missile Crisis (1962)**: The resolution involved secret negotiations where the U.S. agreed to remove missiles from Turkey in exchange for the Soviet Union removing theirs from Cuba.

17. **Welfare Reform (1996)**: President Bill Clinton and a Republican-led Congress compromised on the Personal Responsibility and Work Opportunity Reconciliation Act.

18. **The Affordable Care Act (2010)**: Also known as Obamacare, its

passage involved numerous deals to secure votes from hesitant lawmakers.

19. **The Great Society Programs**: LBJ launched this set of domestic programs to eliminate poverty and racial injustice, which required extensive legislative bargaining.

20. **DACA (Deferred Action for Childhood Arrivals)**: Established in 2012, it resulted from executive action and negotiation amid legislative gridlock on immigration reform.

Great Big Grab Bag of Fun Factoids

1. **Longest-Standing Agreement**: The Jay Treaty 1794, which resolved lingering issues from the American Revolutionary War between the U.S. and Great Britain, lasted until 1803.

2. **Most Controversial Compromise**: The 3/5 Compromise of 1787 was heavily debated and remains a stark reminder of the country's history of slavery and racial inequality.

3. **Quirkiest Deal**: In 1919, the U.S. purchased the Danish West Indies (now the U.S. Virgin Islands) for $25 million in gold, a deal that took decades to finalize.

4. **Nixon's China Deal**: President Richard Nixon's 1972 visit to China opened diplomatic relations between the two countries, a major geopolitical shift achieved through secret negotiations.

5. **Biggest Land Deal**: The Louisiana Purchase in 1803, where the U.S. acquired approximately 827,000 square miles of territory from France for about $15 million, roughly four cents an acre.

With its blend of strategy, negotiation, and occasional humor, political deal-making has profoundly shaped history, influencing everything from territorial boundaries to social policies.

Chapter 12: The Electoral College vs. Popular Vote

Picture this: It's the 1876 presidential election, and the country is embroiled in one of history's most contentious and bizarre electoral disputes. Rutherford B. Hayes, the Republican candidate, is running against Samuel J. Tilden, the Democrat. Tilden wins the popular vote by a significant margin, securing 184 electoral votes to Hayes's 165. But wait, more than 20 electoral votes from Florida, Louisiana, South Carolina, and Oregon are in dispute due to allegations of fraud and intimidation.

Enter the "Compromise of 1877." A special electoral commission consisting of five senators, five representatives, and five Supreme Court justices was set up to resolve the debacle. Despite the intense partisan wrangling, the commission voted along party lines, awarding Hayes all 20 disputed electoral votes, making him the 19th president of the United States. In return, Republicans agreed to withdraw federal troops from the South, effectively ending the Reconstruction era.

This quirky episode is a prime example of the Electoral College's ability to turn what should be a straightforward election into a political circus, leaving many scratching their heads and pondering the sanity of the whole system.

Grab Bag of Useless Helpful Tidbits

1. **Historical Origins**: The Electoral College was established in 1787 as a compromise between electing the president by Congress and by popular vote.
2. **Electors' Role**: Electors are chosen by each state and cast their votes based on the popular vote within their state, though they are not constitutionally bound to do so.
3. **Faithless Electors**: Occasionally, electors vote contrary to their state's popular vote. These "faithless electors" have never altered the outcome of an election.
4. **Population Disparity**: Critics argue the Electoral College gives disproportionate power to less populous states. For instance, Wyoming's electoral vote represents fewer people than California's.
5. **Swing States**: The Electoral College makes certain states, like Florida

and Ohio, crucial battlegrounds, often deciding the election's outcome.

6. **1824 Election**: John Quincy Adams lost the popular vote and the Electoral College but won the presidency after the House of Representatives decided the election.

7. **2000 Election**: George W. Bush lost the popular vote to Al Gore but won the presidency by a narrow margin in the Electoral College, thanks to Florida's contested results.

8. **2016 Election**: Donald Trump lost the popular vote to Hillary Clinton by nearly 3 million votes but won the Electoral College decisively.

9. **Pros of Electoral College**: It prevents a few populated areas from deciding the entire election and encourages a more geographically balanced campaign.

10. **Cons of Electoral College**: It can undermine the principle of "one person, one vote" and lead to the election of a candidate who did not win the popular vote.

11. **National Popular Vote Interstate Compact**: An agreement among some states to award their electoral votes to the national popular vote winner, aiming to circumvent the Electoral College without a constitutional amendment.

12. **Winner-Takes-All System**: Most states use this system, where the candidate with the most votes in a state wins all its electoral votes, further complicating the reflection of the popular vote.

13. **Proportional Allocation**: Maine and Nebraska allocate electoral votes proportionally, but this method is not widely adopted.

14. **Electoral Vote Allocation**: Each state gets electoral votes equal to its total number of senators and representatives, plus three for Washington, D.C.

15. **Potential Reforms**: Proposals include a direct popular vote or a proportional allocation of electoral votes to reflect the national vote accurately.

Great Big Grab Bag of Fun Factoids

1. **Closest Electoral Vote Count**: In the 1960 election, John F. Kennedy won with 303 electoral votes to Richard Nixon's 219, despite a razor-thin popular vote margin.
2. **Largest Electoral Disparity**: 1984 Ronald Reagan won 525 electoral votes to Walter Mondale's 13, despite winning 58.8% of the popular vote.
3. **First Electoral Tie**: The election of 1800 resulted in a tie between Thomas Jefferson and Aaron Burr, resolved by the House of Representatives on the 36th ballot.
4. **Electoral College Size**: There are 538 electoral votes, and a candidate needs 270 to win the presidency.
5. **Faithless Electors Record**: There were a record seven faithless electors in the 2016 election, five of whom pledged to Hillary Clinton and two to Donald Trump.

Chapter 13: The Influence of Lobbyists

In the mid-19th century, the United States Congress was a bustling hive of activity, filled with lawmakers, aides, and lobbyists. One of the most famous lobbyists of the era was Samuel Ward, known as the "King of the Lobby." Ward's most notorious and amusing lobbying effort involved his campaign for the French chef Antoine Carême. Ward wanted Congress to fund a grand culinary exhibition featuring Carême's cooking, promising it would elevate American cuisine to European standards.

Ward hosted elaborate dinners at his home to win over the legislators, showcasing Carême's gourmet creations. Lawmakers were wined with delicacies like vol-au-vent and intricate sugar sculptures, each more extravagant than the last. Ward even staged a dramatic presentation of a pâté à la Carême, claiming it was a revolutionary dish that symbolized Franco-American friendship.

Despite the culinary theatrics and persuasive gastronomy, Congress ultimately declined to fund the exhibition. However, Ward's efforts were not in vain; he succeeded in making his point about the importance of fine dining and secured funding for several smaller culinary projects. His humorous and extravagant lobbying tactics became legendary, highlighting the lengths to which lobbyists will go to achieve their goals.

Grab Bag of Useless Helpful Tidbits

1. **Historical Origins**: The term "lobbyist" originated in the 19th century, referring to people who waited in the lobbies of legislative buildings to speak with lawmakers.

2. **The First Lobbyist**: William Hull is often considered the first professional lobbyist in the U.S., advocating for veterans' benefits in the early 1800s.

3. **Powerful Lobbying Groups**: The National Rifle Association (NRA), AARP, and the American Medical Association (AMA) are some of the most influential lobbying organizations.

4. **K Street**: Known as the heart of the lobbying industry, K Street in Washington, D.C., is home to many lobbying firms and advocacy groups.

5. **The Lobbying Disclosure Act 1995** requires lobbyists to register with Congress and report their activities to ensure transparency.

6. **Revolving Door**: Many former lawmakers and government officials become lobbyists, leveraging their connections and expertise after leaving public service.

7. **Lobbying Expenditures**: Corporations and organizations spend billions of dollars annually on lobbying efforts to influence legislation and policy.

8. **Grassroots Lobbying**: This involves mobilizing the public to contact their representatives, often through campaigns and petitions.

9. **Astroturf Lobbying**: Unlike grassroots lobbying, astroturf lobbying creates the appearance of public support but is orchestrated by interest groups.

10. **Notable Lobbying Efforts**: The American Petroleum Institute successfully lobbied against stringent environmental regulations in the early 2000s.

11. **Controversial Cases**: The Jack Abramoff scandal in the early 2000s exposed widespread corruption and led to significant reforms in lobbying practices.

12. **Lobbying and Healthcare**: The healthcare industry, including pharmaceutical companies, is one of the biggest spenders on lobbying in the U.S.
13. **Tech Industry Lobbying**: In recent years, companies like Google, Amazon, and Facebook have ramped up their lobbying efforts to influence tech policy and regulation.
14. **Foreign Influence**: Foreign governments often hire lobbyists to promote their interests and improve relations with U.S. policymakers.
15. **Lobbying in State Governments**: Lobbying is not limited to the federal level; state governments also see significant lobbying activity.
16. **Ethics Rules**: Strict rules govern lobbyists' interactions with lawmakers, including gift bans and disclosure requirements.
17. **Lobbying Techniques**: Lobbyists use various methods, such as direct lobbying, coalition building, and public relations campaigns, to sway opinion and policy.
18. **PACs and Super PACs**: Political Action Committees and Super PACs raise and spend money to support candidates and causes, often working closely with lobbyists.
19. **Lobbying and Legislation**: Lobbyists are key in drafting legislation, providing lawmakers with information and expertise on complex issues.
20. **Lobbying and Public Perception**: While lobbying is a legitimate part of the political process, the public views it skeptically due to concerns about undue influence and corruption.

Great Big Grab Bag of Fun Factoids

1. **Most Money Spent**: In 2020, the pharmaceutical industry spent over $306 million on lobbying, the highest of any industry.
2. **Unusual Campaigns**: 2008 the American Mustache Institute lobbied for a tax deduction for mustache grooming expenses, calling it the "Stimulus To Allow Critical Hair Expenses" (STACHE) Act.
3. **Longest Lobbying Campaign**: The Prohibition repeal lobby worked for 13 years to overturn the 18th Amendment, ultimately succeeding in 1933 with the 21st Amendment.

4. **Lobbying for Holidays**: Lobbyists have successfully advocated establishing national holidays, including Martin Luther King Jr. Day and Earth Day.

5. **Big Tobacco**: The tobacco industry's lobbying efforts in the 20th century were some of the most extensive and controversial, involving misinformation campaigns to downplay the health risks of smoking.

Chapter 14: Political Symbols and Traditions

Once upon a time, in 1884, the Democratic National Convention was in full swing in Chicago. Amidst the chaos, a peculiar tradition began with Alonzo "Lon" Chapin. Lon, a dedicated supporter of Grover Cleveland, was known for his eccentric habit of carrying a large, inflatable donkey to political rallies. As he paraded around the convention with his inflatable companion, Lon's donkey quickly became the center of attention, drawing laughter and cheers from the delegates.

The spectacle caught the eye of political cartoonist Thomas Nast, who had previously popularized the donkey as a symbol for the Democratic Party. Inspired by the sight of Lon and his inflatable friend, Nast sketched a humorous cartoon featuring the donkey as the steadfast, albeit stubborn, mascot of the Democrats. The cartoon was an instant hit, solidifying the donkey's place in American political symbolism.

Lon's inflatable donkey may have been a quirky addition to the convention but left a lasting legacy. From that point forward, the donkey became a beloved, if sometimes mocked, emblem of the Democratic Party, a tradition born out of one man's eccentricity and a cartoonist's wit.

Grab Bag of Useless Helpful Tidbits

1. **The Democratic Donkey**: The Democratic Party's donkey symbol originated from a political cartoon by Thomas Nast in the 1870s.

2. **The Republican Elephant**: The Republican Party's elephant symbol, which came from a Thomas Nast cartoon, represents the party's strength and dignity.

3. **Uncle Sam**: Uncle Sam became a national symbol during the War of 1812, personifying the U.S. government, and was popularized in recruitment posters during World War I.
4. **Stars and Stripes**: The American flag, with its stars and stripes, was officially adopted on June 14, 1777, now celebrated as Flag Day.
5. **The Presidential Seal**: The presidential seal features an eagle holding an olive branch and arrows, symbolizing peace and readiness for war.
6. **Hail to the Chief**: This song has been the official anthem played to announce the arrival of the U.S. president since the early 19th century.
7. **National Anthem**: "The Star-Spangled Banner," written by Francis Scott Key during the War of 1812, became the national anthem in 1931.
8. **The Pledge of Allegiance**: Originally written in 1892, Congress officially adopted the Pledge of Allegiance in 1942.
9. **Inaugural Bible**: Many presidents have taken their oath of office on the Lincoln Bible, first used by Abraham Lincoln in 1861.
10. **White House Easter Egg Roll**: This annual event on the White House lawn dates back to 1878 during Rutherford B. Hayes's presidency.
11. **State of the Union**: The State of the Union address, mandated by the Constitution, has evolved from a written report to a televised speech.
12. **Presidential Turkey Pardon**: The tradition of pardoning a Thanksgiving turkey dates back to the 1940s and was formalized by George H.W. Bush in 1989.
13. **The Rose Garden**: The White House Rose Garden, established by First Lady Ellen Wilson in 1913, is often used for official announcements and ceremonies.
14. **National Mall**: The National Mall in Washington, D.C., has numerous monuments and memorials, symbolizing American history and ideals.
15. **Mount Rushmore**: This iconic monument features the faces of four U.S. presidents, representing the nation's birth, growth, development, and preservation.
16. **The Liberty Bell**: Located in Philadelphia, symbolizes American

independence and freedom despite its infamous crack.

17. **Fourth of July**: Independence Day, celebrated on July 4th, marks the adoption of the Declaration of Independence in 1776.

18. **The Great Seal**: The Great Seal of the United States, used on official documents, features an eagle and the motto "E Pluribus Unum" (Out of Many, One).

19. **Capitol Rotunda**: The Rotunda of the U.S. Capitol symbolizes American democracy and is often used for lying in state ceremonies.

20. **Electoral College**: Established by the Constitution, the Electoral College is a unique method of electing the president, symbolizing the federal nature of the U.S. government.

Great Big Grab Bag of Fun Factoids

1. **Presidential Turkey Pardon**: The first unofficial turkey pardon dates back to Abraham Lincoln, who spared a turkey at his son's request. The formal tradition began with George H.W. Bush in 1989.

2. **Inaugural Ball**: The first inaugural ball was held for James Madison in 1809, setting a tradition for celebratory events on inauguration day.

3. **Longest National Anthem**: "The Star-Spangled Banner" has four verses, but only the first is commonly sung. The entire anthem is quite lengthy, at 32 lines.

4. **Flag Folding**: The 13 folds of the American flag during military funerals each have symbolic meanings, representing principles of American life.

5. **National Bird**: The bald eagle was chosen as the national bird in 1782, despite Benjamin Franklin's preference for the turkey, which he considered a more respectable bird.

Chapter 15: Political Oddities and Surprises

In the annals of political oddities, few events rival the election of 1928 in Muncie, Indiana. As the story goes on, a charismatic yet unconventional candidate named Zephyr McCorkle decides to run for mayor. Zephyr, known for his eccentricity, promised to turn the town into a bustling hub of prosperity through an elaborate scheme involving pigeon racing. Yes, you read that correctly—pigeon racing.

His campaign slogan, "A Pigeon in Every Pot," became the talk of the town. Zephyr held rallies where he released flocks of pigeons into the air, much to the amusement and bewilderment of the townsfolk. Despite his outlandish platform, Zephyr's infectious enthusiasm and flair for showmanship won over the hearts of many voters.

When election day arrived, the town was abuzz with anticipation. In a shocking twist, Zephyr McCorkle won by a landslide, becoming the mayor of Muncie. Unfortunately, his grand plans for pigeon-powered prosperity never took flight, and his term was marked by more humorous antics than actual governance. Nonetheless, Zephyr's improbable victory remains a cherished tale of political surprise and spectacle in Muncie's history.

Grab Bag of Useless Helpful Tidbits

1. **Unplanned Political Careers**: Harry S. Truman became vice president and then president without ever actively seeking office. He was chosen as FDR's running mate in a last-minute deal.

2. **Surprising Election Outcomes**: In 1948, despite all polls predicting his defeat, Harry S. Truman won the presidential election against Thomas Dewey. He famously held up a newspaper with the incorrect headline "Dewey Defeats Truman."

3. **Accidental President**: Gerald Ford became president in 1974 without being elected to the presidency or vice presidency, following the resignation of Richard Nixon and Spiro Agnew.

4. **Jesse Ventura**: Former professional wrestler Jesse Ventura won the Minnesota gubernatorial race in 1998, running as a third-party candidate and shocking the political establishment.

5. **Unexpected Senator**: Comedian Al Franken won a U.S. Senate seat in Minnesota in 2008, transitioning from comedy to politics with surprising success.

6. **Bizarre Political Predictions**: In 1840, astrologer Richard Adams Locke predicted William Henry Harrison's election and subsequent

death in office, which eerily came true.

7. **Calvin Coolidge's Silence**: Known for his reticence, President Calvin Coolidge once famously responded to a dinner bet by saying only "You lose" to a woman who wagered she could get him to say more than two words.

8. **Lost to a Dead Man**: In 2000, Missouri Governor Mel Carnahan won a U.S. Senate seat despite having died in a plane crash three weeks before the election. His widow served in his place.

9. **Political Cartoon Influences**: Political cartoons have sometimes dramatically swayed public opinion, such as Thomas Nast's cartoons bringing down New York City's corrupt Tammany Hall.

10. **Unexpected Resignation**: In 1973, Vice President Spiro Agnew resigned after being charged with tax evasion, a rare and unexpected departure from office.

11. **The Shoe Incident**: In 1960, Soviet Premier Nikita Khrushchev famously banged his shoe on a desk at the United Nations to make a point, shocking attendees.

12. **Surprise Endorsements**: In 2008, former Secretary of State Colin Powell's endorsement of Barack Obama was unexpected and influential in the election.

13. **Impeachment Acquittals**: Both Andrew Johnson and Bill Clinton were impeached by the House but acquitted by the Senate, surprising many who expected their removal from office.

14. **Running from Prison**: In 1920, socialist candidate Eugene V. Debs ran for president from prison, where he was serving a sentence for anti-war activities, and received nearly a million votes.

15. **Write-In Victories**: In 1954, Strom Thurmond won a U.S. Senate seat in South Carolina as a write-in candidate, the first such victory in history.

16. **Political Comebacks**: Richard Nixon's return to politics in 1968 after losing the presidency in 1960 and the California gubernatorial race in 1962 was a surprising political comeback.

17. **Odd Presidential Pets**: President Calvin Coolidge had a pet raccoon named Rebecca, originally intended to be part of Thanksgiving dinner.

18. **Youngest Congressman**: Jed Johnson Jr., who was elected to the U.S. House of Representatives in 1964 at the age of 24, is the youngest person ever to hold office in Congress.
19. **First Female Vice President Candidate**: Geraldine Ferraro made history as the first female vice-presidential candidate on a major party ticket in 1984, running with Walter Mondale.
20. **The Longest Filibuster**: Senator Strom Thurmond holds the record for the longest solo filibuster in history, speaking for 24 hours and 18 minutes against the Civil Rights Act of 1957.

Great Big Grab Bag of Fun Factoids

1. **Youngest Mayor**: In 2018, Michael Tubbs, then 26, became the youngest mayor of Stockton, California.
2. **Smallest Election Margin**: In 2000, Al Gore won the popular vote by approximately 540,000 but lost the Electoral College to George W. Bush by just 537 votes in Florida.
3. **Oddest Political Debate**: The 1960 Kennedy-Nixon debate was the first televised presidential debate. Those who listened on the radio thought Nixon had won, while TV viewers favored Kennedy.
4. **First Televised Inauguration**: Harry S. Truman's inauguration in 1949 was the first to be televised, bringing the ceremony into American living rooms nationwide.
5. **First Presidential Library**: Franklin D. Roosevelt established the first presidential library in 1941, setting a tradition for archiving presidential documents and memorabilia.

Chapter 16: The Role of Technology in Politics

In the early days of the internet, political campaigns were just beginning to explore the potential of this new technology. During the 1992 presidential campaign, Bill Clinton's team decided to experiment with email. They set up an email address where supporters could send messages, thinking it would be a great way to connect with voters. However, they didn't anticipate the volume of emails or the kinds of messages they would receive.

One day, a campaign volunteer checked the inbox and found it flooded with messages, many of which were from an enthusiastic but eccentric supporter named Larry. Larry sent daily emails with suggestions ranging from serious policy proposals to absurd ideas, like replacing the national anthem with "Achy Breaky Heart" by Billy Ray Cyrus. One email even included a detailed plan for a "Presidential Pet Talent Show," complete with a judging panel of celebrity animals.

While the campaign never implemented Larry's suggestions, they couldn't help but appreciate his creativity and enthusiasm. The incident highlighted the uncharted waters of digital campaigning and the unexpected ways technology could connect (and amuse) candidates and voters alike.

Grab Bag of Useless Helpful Tidbits

1. **Social Media Influence**: Social media platforms like Twitter, Facebook, and Instagram have become crucial tools for political campaigns, allowing direct communication with voters.
2. **First Internet Campaign**: Bill Clinton's and Al Gore's 1996 presidential campaign was the first to use a campaign website to reach voters.
3. **Email Fundraising**: Howard Dean's 2004 presidential campaign revolutionized fundraising by using email to solicit small donations from many supporters.
4. **Data Analytics**: Barack Obama's 2008 campaign used advanced data analytics to target voters and optimize campaign strategies, setting a new standard for digital campaigning.
5. **Cybersecurity Threats**: The 2016 presidential election highlighted the importance of cybersecurity, with concerns over hacking and misinformation spreading online.
6. **Digital Advertising**: Political campaigns now spend millions on digital advertising, targeting specific demographics with tailored messages.
7. **Mobile Apps**: Campaigns use mobile apps to engage supporters,

provide updates, and facilitate grassroots organizing.

8. **Online Petitions**: Digital platforms like Change.org have made it easier for citizens to start and sign petitions, influencing political decisions.

9. **Live Streaming**: Politicians use live streaming on social media to broadcast events and speeches in real time, reaching a broader audience.

10. **Viral Campaigns**: Memes and viral videos have become a staple of modern campaigns, often used to generate buzz and engage younger voters.

11. **Virtual Town Halls**: Politicians hold virtual town halls to interact with constituents, especially when in-person events are not feasible.

12. **Blockchain Voting**: Some experts advocate for blockchain technology to secure electronic voting systems and ensure the integrity of election results.

13. **AI and Chatbots**: Campaigns use AI and chatbots to answer voter questions, provide information, and gather data on voter preferences.

14. **Social Media Bots**: The use of bots to spread political messages and influence public opinion is a growing concern in the digital age.

15. **Geofencing**: Campaigns use geofencing to target smartphone ads within specific geographic areas, such as rally locations or polling places.

16. **Big Data**: Campaigns analyze vast amounts of data from various sources to refine strategies and predict voter behavior.

17. **Digital Campaign Merchandise**: Online stores selling campaign merchandise have become a significant source of revenue and promotion.

18. **Crowdsourcing Ideas**: Politicians sometimes use social media to crowdsource policy ideas and engage with the public on policy development.

19. **Fact-Checking Websites**: Sites like FactCheck.org and Snopes help combat misinformation by verifying claims made by politicians and political ads.

20. **Deepfakes**: The rise of deepfake technology poses a new challenge, as it can create realistic but fake videos that can be used to mislead

voters.

Great Big Grab Bag of Fun Factoids

1. **First Campaign Website**: Bill Clinton and Al Gore launched the first presidential campaign website in 1996, marking the beginning of digital campaigning.
2. **Most-Followed Politicians**: As of 2024, Barack Obama remains one of the most-followed politicians on Twitter, with over 133 million followers.
3. **Obama's 2008 MySpace Page**: During his 2008 campaign, Barack Obama had an official MySpace page, reflecting the early use of social media in campaigns.
4. **First Tweet by a U.S. President**: In 2009, Barack Obama sent the first tweet by a sitting U.S. president using the official @POTUS account.
5. **Virtual Reality**: In 2016, Bernie Sanders' campaign created a 360-degree virtual reality video to give supporters a front-row seat at his rallies, pioneering the use of VR in campaigns.

Chapter 17: Political Careers and Pathways

In the annals of American politics, few stories are as delightfully odd as that of Stephen Bullock, a mild-mannered librarian from Vermont. In 1982, Bullock's friends convinced him to run for the state legislature as a joke. Known for his eccentric collection of antique buttons and a knack for reciting obscure historical facts, Bullock seemed an unlikely candidate.

Deciding to embrace the prank, Bullock ran a whimsical campaign, promising to rename Vermont's cows and institute a "Button Day" holiday. His slogans included, "Vote Bullock: Because why not?" and "A chicken in every pot, a button on every shirt!" To everyone's surprise, including his own, Bullock's quirky charm and genuine enthusiasm won over voters tired of traditional politics.

The joke turned serious on election night as Bullock won by a comfortable margin. His victory speech, delivered while wearing a button-covered vest, became legendary: "I may not have all the answers, but I have plenty of buttons!" Despite his unconventional start, Bullock served three terms, championing local libraries and historic preservation. His story remains a testament to the unpredictable nature of political careers and the power of authenticity and humor.

Grab Bag of Useless Helpful Tidbits

1. **Career Politicians**: Career politicians often start at local levels, such as city councils or state legislatures, and gradually move to higher offices.
2. **Political Newcomers**: Political newcomers, often from diverse professional backgrounds, can bring fresh perspectives and challenge established norms.
3. **Grassroots Beginnings**: Many politicians start their careers through grassroots activism and community organizing before running for office.
4. **Military Service**: Numerous politicians, such as John McCain and Tammy Duckworth, began their careers with military service, leveraging their leadership experience.
5. **Lawyers in Politics**: Law is a common precursor to a political career, providing skills in legislation, negotiation, and public speaking.
6. **Business to Politics**: Business leaders like Michael Bloomberg and Donald Trump have transitioned to politics, often emphasizing their management skills.
7. **Educators in Office**: Educators like Elizabeth Warren use their academic experience to inform policy and connect with constituents on education issues.
8. **Political Mentors**: Famous political figures often mentor newcomers like Senator Ted Kennedy, who mentored Obama during his early Senate years.
9. **Family Dynasties**: Political families, like the Kennedys, Bushes, and Clintons, often see multiple members hold public office across generations.

10. **Unexpected Shifts**: Ronald Reagan's shift from Hollywood actor to governor of California and then president is one of the most famous career changes.

11. **Young Politicians**: Alexandria Ocasio-Cortez was elected to Congress at 29, highlighting the increasing influence of younger politicians.

12. **Late Bloomers**: Strom Thurmond began his Senate career at 52 and served until he was 100, showcasing the longevity of political careers.

13. **Activists to Politicians**: Many civil rights activists, like John Lewis, transitioned from activism to long political careers.

14. **Celebrity Politicians**: Celebrities such as Arnold Schwarzenegger and Clint Eastwood have successfully run for political office, leveraging their fame.

15. **Women's Pathways**: Women in politics often face unique challenges and bring different perspectives, with trailblazers like Shirley Chisholm paving the way.

16. **Career Stumbles**: Richard Nixon's career saw dramatic ups and downs, from losing the California gubernatorial race to winning the presidency and resigning.

17. **Educational Backgrounds**: Politicians often hold degrees in political science, law, or public administration, but some, like Harry Truman, had minimal formal education.

18. **Civic Engagement**: Involvement in local civic organizations or boards is a common stepping stone to elected office.

19. **Tech-savvy Politicians**: The rise of technology has seen a new breed of tech-savvy politicians who effectively use digital platforms to campaign and govern.

20. **International Influences**: Some U.S. politicians have international diplomacy or business backgrounds, bringing global perspectives to domestic policy.

Great Big Grab Bag of Fun Factoids

1. **Youngest Politician**: Saira Blair was elected to the West Virginia House of Delegates in 2014 at 18, making her the youngest state

    lawmaker in U.S. history.

2. **Oldest Politician**: Strom Thurmond served in the U.S. Senate until he was 100, making him the oldest serving senator.
3. **Most Surprising Career Shift**: Ronald Reagan went from being a Hollywood actor to the governor of California and then to the president of the United States.
4. **Political Cartoonist Turned Politician**: Thomas Nast, famous for his political cartoons, was considered for the U.S. consulship in Ecuador, showcasing a unique career pivot.
5. **From Astronaut to Politician**: John Glenn, the first American to orbit Earth, later became a U.S. Senator, illustrating a remarkable shift from space exploration to politics.

Chapter 18: International Perspectives on American Politics

In the late 1950s, a small village in Italy called Candido Godi decided to hold its American presidential election. The quirky and somewhat cheeky idea came from the town's mayor, who wanted to foster a sense of global citizenship among the villagers. They set up voting booths and distributed ballots with the names of the actual U.S. presidential candidates. They even hosted debates where locals impersonating the candidates presented their platforms (complete with over-the-top accents and exaggerated gestures).

On election day, the villagers turned out in droves, enthusiastically casting their votes. The results were tallied, and the winner was announced with much fanfare: the villagers had overwhelmingly elected their version of Dwight D. Eisenhower. The village's mock election gained international media attention, with reporters worldwide descending on the tiny town to cover the story. It was a delightful example of how American politics could capture the imagination of people far beyond U.S. borders, even if it were through a humorous and light-hearted lens.

Grab Bag of Useless Helpful Tidbits

1. **Global Media Coverage**: International media closely follow American elections, often with live broadcasts and detailed analysis.
2. **Alliances and Influence**: The United States maintains key alliances with countries like the United Kingdom, Canada, and Japan, which closely monitor U.S. political shifts.
3. **Soft Power**: American culture, through movies, music, and television, significantly influences global perceptions of U.S. politics.
4. **Foreign Influence**: Countries like Russia and China have been accused of trying to influence U.S. elections through cyber-attacks and disinformation campaigns.
5. **Economic Ties**: The U.S. economic policies have a global impact, affecting international trade and financial markets.
6. **NATO Relations**: NATO allies often view U.S. presidential elections with concern, especially regarding defense commitments and international cooperation.
7. **Environmental Policies**: U.S. stances on climate change and environmental regulations significantly influence international views on American politics.
8. **Human Rights**: International bodies scrutinize U.S. policies on human rights and can influence global standards.
9. **Immigration Policies**: Changes in U.S. immigration laws can have ripple effects globally, influencing migration patterns and international relations.
10. **United Nations**: The U.S.'s role in the UN is pivotal, with its policies often shaping international resolutions and peacekeeping efforts.
11. **Cultural Diplomacy**: American ambassadors and cultural programs promote U.S. values abroad, influencing how American politics are perceived.
12. **Global Protests**: Major U.S. political events like the 2020 Black Lives Matter protests often inspire similar movements worldwide.
13. **Economic Sanctions**: U.S. sanctions on countries like Iran and North Korea are closely watched and debated internationally.
14. **Technological Impact**: American tech companies influence political discourse globally through platforms like Facebook and Twitter.
15. **Educational Influence**: U.S. universities attract international

students, who often become influential in their home countries and maintain a keen interest in American politics.

16. **Cultural Exchange Programs**: Programs like the Fulbright Scholarship foster international understanding of U.S. politics and culture.

17. **Diplomatic Reactions**: International leaders often comment on U.S. elections, reflecting their stakes in the outcome.

18. **Public Opinion Polls**: Surveys show that global public opinion on U.S. leadership can vary widely, often reflecting the policies of the incumbent administration.

19. **American Exceptionalism**: The concept of American exceptionalism is both admired and critiqued internationally, influencing how U.S. actions are perceived.

20. **Foreign Lobbying**: Foreign governments and organizations sometimes lobby U.S. politicians to influence policies that affect their interests.

Great Big Grab Bag of Fun Factoids

1. **Most Influenced**: Canada is one of the countries most influenced by American politics due to its geographical proximity and strong economic ties.

2. **Least Influenced**: Countries with limited diplomatic or economic ties to the U.S., such as North Korea, are less influenced by American politics.

3. **Notable Commentators**: British journalist Alistair Cooke's "Letter from America" was a famous radio series that provided insightful commentary on American life and politics for over 50 years.

4. **French Perspective**: French intellectuals and politicians often provide a critical yet keenly interested perspective on U.S. politics, reflecting a mix of admiration and rivalry.

5. **International Elections**: Some countries, like Germany, have seen local political movements inspired by American campaigns adopting similar strategies and slogans.

Chapter 19: Ethics in Politics

In 1957, the small town of Springfield was rocked by a political scandal that would go down in history as "The Great Springfield Cheese Caper." Mayor Elmer "Big Cheese" Thompson, known for his love of dairy products, was at the center of an ethical debacle. It all started when a local cheese manufacturer donated a giant wheel of cheddar to the mayor's re-election campaign. Instead of reporting the gift as required by law, Mayor Thompson decided to keep the cheese for himself.

Things got cheesy when the mayor threw a lavish party featuring the enormous cheddar as the centerpiece. When the press got wind of the unreported gift, they sniffed out the scandal, dubbing it "Cheddar-gate." The town was abuzz with cheese puns and jokes, and Mayor Thompson's popularity melted away faster than a slice of Swiss on a hot day.

Facing intense scrutiny and public ridicule, Mayor Thompson confessed, "I was just trying to spread some cheesy goodwill!" He was fined for the ethics violation, and while he lost the next election, the town of Springfield gained a hilarious chapter in its political history. The Great Springfield Cheese Caper remains an excellent example of why transparency is crucial in politics.

Grab Bag of Useless Helpful Tidbits

1. **Teapot Dome Scandal**: One of the most notorious early 20th-century scandals involving oil reserve leases and significant bribery exposed corruption in the Harding administration.
2. **Watergate**: The break-in at the Democratic National Committee headquarters and subsequent cover-up led to President Nixon's resignation and widespread ethics reforms.
3. **Iran-Contra Affair**: This 1980s scandal involved secret arms sales to Iran and the illegal funding of Contra rebels in Nicaragua, leading to several convictions.
4. **Lobbying Disclosure Act of 1995**: Enacted to increase transparency in lobbying activities, requiring lobbyists to register and report their activities.

5. **Ethics in Government Act of 1978**: Passed in the wake of Watergate, this act established mandatory public disclosure of public officials' financial and employment histories.

6. **Senate Ethics Committee**: Established to investigate and take action on ethical breaches by senators.

7. **House Ethics Committee**: This committee handles ethical issues in the House of Representatives, ensuring members adhere to rules and standards.

8. **Citizens United v. FEC**: This Supreme Court decision allowed for unlimited corporate spending in elections, raising ethical concerns about influence and transparency.

9. **Stock Act of 2012**: Prohibits insider trading by members of Congress and other government employees.

10. **Pay-to-Play Scandals**: Instances where political donations are exchanged for political favors or contracts, leading to widespread corruption allegations.

11. **Campaign Finance Reform**: Efforts to limit money's influence in politics, such as the McCain-Feingold Act, aim to address ethical issues in campaign funding.

12. **Whistleblower Protections**: Laws that protect individuals who expose unethical or illegal activities within the government.

13. **Nepotism Laws**: Regulations that prevent public officials from appointing relatives to governmental positions.

14. **Ethical Dilemmas**: Policy-making often involves complex ethical choices, such as balancing national security with individual privacy rights.

15. **Conflict of Interest**: Politicians must avoid situations where personal interests conflict with public duties.

16. **Gift Bans**: Many government bodies have rules limiting or banning gifts to public officials to prevent undue influence.

17. **Financial Disclosure**: Public officials must disclose their financial interests to ensure transparency and prevent corruption.

18. **Bribery Laws**: Strict laws exist to prevent and punish bribery of public officials, ensuring decisions are made in the public interest.

19. **Revolving Door**: The movement of individuals between government

positions and private sector jobs can raise ethical questions about influence and insider knowledge.

20. **Ethics Training**: Many governmental bodies require ethics training for employees to promote understanding and compliance with ethical standards.

Great Big Grab Bag of Fun Factoids

1. **Most Significant Ethical Reform**: The Ethics in Government Act of 1978, which established the Office of Government Ethics, is one of the most significant reforms in American political history.
2. **Notorious Ethical Breach**: The Teapot Dome Scandal remains one of the most infamous examples of government corruption involving high-level officials and vast sums of money.
3. **Whistleblower Fame**: Mark Felt, known as "Deep Throat," was the whistleblower who exposed the Watergate scandal, leading to President Nixon's resignation.
4. **Public Office Financial Disclosures**: The STOCK Act requires public officials to disclose financial transactions within 45 days, increasing transparency.
5. **Ethics Committee Censure**: In 1989, House Speaker Jim Wright resigned amid an ethics investigation, making it one of the highest-profile ethical cases in congressional history.

Chapter 20: Political Satire and Humor

In 1968, Dick Tuck, a political prankster known for his satirical jabs at opponents, orchestrated one of his most famous stunts. During Richard Nixon's campaign, Tuck hired a pregnant woman to wander through a crowd holding a sign that read, "Nixon's the One." When asked about his loss in the 1966 California State Senate race, Tuck famously quipped, "The people have spoken, the bastards."

Grab Bag of Useless Helpful Tidbits

1. **Mark Twain's Sharp Wit**: Mark Twain is often considered one of the pioneers of American political satire. His quips and essays frequently lampooned politicians and policies of his time.
2. **Will Rogers' Influence**: An early 20th-century humorist, Will Rogers poked fun at the political landscape in his newspaper columns and radio broadcasts, making him a beloved figure in American homes.
3. **"The Daily Show"**: Jon Stewart's tenure on "The Daily Show" transformed it into a significant platform for political satire, influencing public opinion and spawning a new generation of satirists.
4. **"Saturday Night Live"**: Since its inception in 1975, "SNL" has skewered politicians from all parties, becoming a staple of American political humor.
5. **"The Colbert Report"**: Stephen Colbert's persona as a conservative pundit brilliantly parodied the format and rhetoric of cable news shows, adding a layer of satire to honest political discourse.
6. **Thomas Nast's Cartoons**: In the 19th century, Thomas Nast's editorial cartoons in Harper's Weekly played a significant role in shaping public perceptions of political figures like Boss Tweed and the Tammany Hall political machine.
7. **"Doonesbury" Comic Strip**: Garry Trudeau's "Doonesbury" has been a consistent source of political satire in newspaper comics since 1970.
8. **Political Roast Traditions**: Events like the White House Correspondents' Dinner feature comedic roasts of politicians, blending humor with political critique.
9. **The Impact of "South Park"**: Known for its irreverence, "South Park" often tackles political issues with a blend of crude humor and sharp satire.
10. **Satirical News Websites**: Platforms like "The Onion" provide satirical takes on current events, often blurring the line between reality and parody.
11. **Voltaire's Legacy**: The tradition of political satire can be traced back to writers like Voltaire, whose works mocked his time's political and

religious authorities.

12. **Modern Memes**: Social media has given rise to political memes, which often use humor to comment on and critique political events and figures.

13. **"Yes, Minister" and "Yes, Prime Minister"**: These British TV series offer a humorous look at the inner workings of government, resonating with American audiences as well.

14. **The Role of Cartoons**: Political cartoons remain a powerful medium for satire, condensing complex issues into a single, often humorous, image.

15. **"Veep"**: The TV show "Veep" provides a comedic yet insightful look at the absurdities and challenges of American politics.

16. **Late-Night Monologues**: Hosts like Johnny Carson, David Letterman, and more recently, John Oliver and Trevor Noah have used their platforms to deliver biting political commentary under the guise of humor.

17. **"Full Frontal with Samantha Bee"**: This show combines satire with investigative journalism, offering a unique perspective on current events.

18. **Impact on Public Perception**: Studies have shown that political satire can influence viewers' opinions and increase their political engagement.

19. **Satire as a Coping Mechanism**: During political turmoil, satire often serves as a way for the public to process and critique the issues.

20. **Historical Roots**: Political satire has deep historical roots, with examples in ancient Greek plays, Roman literature, and beyond.

Great Big Grab Bag of Fun Factoids

1. **Longest-Running Satirical Show**: "Saturday Night Live" holds the record for the longest-running satirical television show, having been on the air since 1975.

2. **The Impact of a Joke**: In 1975, Chevy Chase's impression of Gerald Ford as a bumbling klutz on "SNL" contributed to the public's perception of Ford as accident-prone.

3. **Jon Stewart's Influence**: A 2004 study found that viewers of "The Daily Show" with Jon Stewart were better informed about political issues than those who watched traditional news programs.
4. **Voltaire's "Candide"**: Published in 1759, Candide is one of the earliest and most famous works of political satire. It uses humor to criticize the optimism of Enlightenment philosophers.
5. **"The Colbert Bump"** refers to the increase in popularity or support that politicians and authors experienced after appearing on "The Colbert Report."

Chapter 21: Term Limits in Politics

One of the most humorous stories about a politician overstaying their welcome involves the incredibly long tenure of Congressman John Dingell. Serving as a U.S. Representative for Michigan for nearly 60 years, Dingell became a legendary figure in American politics.

Known for his sharp wit and unwavering dedication, Dingell's career spanned multiple generations of lawmakers, making him a constant presence in the House of Representatives. His lengthy service often led to jokes and lighthearted jabs, but it also sparked serious discussions about the need for term limits to prevent such prolonged tenures.

Despite the humor, Dingell's career highlighted the challenges of political reform and the difficulty of balancing experience with the need for fresh perspectives. His story is a prime example of why many advocate for term limits to ensure political renewal and prevent the entrenchment of career politicians.

Grab Bag of Useless Helpful Tidbits

1. **Origins of Term Limits**: Term limits have been a topic of debate since the founding of the United States. The Founding Fathers initially debated them, with the Articles of Confederation limiting congressional service but the Constitution omitting such restrictions.
2. **Presidential Term Limits**: The 22nd Amendment, ratified in 1951, directly responded to Franklin D. Roosevelt's unprecedented four-

term presidency. It limits presidents to two terms or a maximum of ten years if they assumed office via succession.

3. **Congressional Term Limits**: While there are no federal term limits for Congress, the idea has been proposed many times. Proponents argue it prevents career politicians from becoming disconnected from their constituents, while opponents believe it removes experienced legislators from office.

4. **Term Limits Around the World:** Many countries have term limits for their leaders. For example, Mexico limits its president to a single six-year term, while Russia's term limits have been notably flexible, allowing Vladimir Putin to maintain power through various means.

5. **Famous Politicians Affected**: Bill Clinton and George W. Bush had to step down after their second terms due to the 22nd Amendment.

6. **Pros and Cons**: Supporters of term limits argue they prevent corruption, encourage fresh ideas, and keep politicians connected to the people. Critics counter that term limits lead to a loss of experienced leaders and increase the influence of lobbyists and unelected officials.

7. **Exceptions and Loopholes**: Some politicians have found creative ways to extend their influence. For example, New York City Mayor Michael Bloomberg successfully campaigned to expand the city's term limit law so he could run for a third term.

8. **Public Opinion**: Surveys generally strongly support term limits. A 2013 Gallup poll found that 75% of Americans supported term limits for Congress.

9. **Impact on Legislative Effectiveness**: Critics argue that term limits can reduce legislative effectiveness by removing experienced lawmakers who understand the complexities of the legislative process.

10. **Term Limits in State Governments**: Many U.S. states have imposed term limits on their governors and legislators, which has had varying impacts on state governance.

11. **Career Politicians**: Many politicians spend their entire careers in public office, claiming to understand middle-class struggles despite never having a job outside politics. Examples include Joe Biden and Mitch McConnell.

12. **Term Limits and Political Accountability**: Proponents argue that term limits increase political accountability by regularly introducing new candidates who must appeal to voters without relying on incumbency.

13. **Historical Debates**: The idea of term limits has been debated throughout U.S. history, with figures like Thomas Jefferson advocating for rotation in office to prevent tyranny.

14. **Modern Advocacy for Term Limits**: Organizations like U.S. Term Limits continue to advocate for implementing term limits at all levels of government.

15. **Term Limits and Political Diversity**: Some argue that term limits can increase political diversity by allowing more candidates to run for office and bringing new perspectives to governance.

16. **Term Limits and Corruption**: Studies have shown mixed results on whether term limits reduce corruption, with some evidence suggesting that inexperienced legislators may be more susceptible to influence.

17. **International Examples**: Countries like France and South Korea have implemented term limits for their presidents, reflecting a global trend toward limiting the tenure of executive leaders.

18. **The Role of Term Limits in Democracies:** Term limits are seen as a safeguard in democracies to prevent the concentration of power and ensure regular leadership changes.

19. **Term Limits in Local Governments**: Many U.S. cities and counties have adopted term limits for their mayors and council members, with varying degrees of success and public approval.

20. **The Future of Term Limits**: The debate over term limits continues, with some advocating for reforms to enhance political accountability and others warning of unintended consequences.

Great Big Grab Bag of Fun Factoids

1. **Longest-Serving Politicians**: Some politicians have served impressively long tenures despite term limits. John Dingell served in the House of Representatives for over 59 years, the longest in U.S.

history.

2. **Historical Controversies**: The most notable controversy surrounding term limits was FDR's four terms. This led directly to the 22nd Amendment, highlighting how one individual's extended tenure can reshape constitutional law.

3. **Amusing Loopholes**: Russian President Vladimir Putin has navigated term limits by alternating between the presidency and the prime minister, effectively maintaining control over the country since 1999.

4. **Career Politicians**: Many politicians have spent their entire careers in public office, often claiming to understand middle-class struggles despite never having a job outside politics. For instance, Joe Biden has been in public office since 1973, and Mitch McConnell since 1985, making them quintessential career politicians.

5. **Public Service Claims**: Some career politicians, like Nancy Pelosi and Chuck Schumer, have been in public service for decades. Despite their extensive tenure, they often portray themselves as champions of the middle class, leading to criticism and satire about their accurate understanding of ordinary citizens' lives.

Chapter 22: The Economics of Politics

In 2009, U.S. Senator John Kerry made headlines for an amusingly unexpected financial disclosure that showcased politicians' wealth and sometimes surprising fiscal maneuvers. Despite being known for his significant wealth, partially derived from marrying into the Heinz ketchup fortune, Kerry found himself at the center of a humorous controversy. He failed to pay $500,000 in taxes on his luxurious yacht, the Isabel, by docking it in Rhode Island instead of his home state of Massachusetts. Rhode Island, unlike Massachusetts, did not impose a sales tax on yachts, saving Kerry a significant sum.

However, when the story broke, it quickly spiraled into a public relations debacle, combining public outrage over the apparent tax evasion with a certain degree of amusement at how even the wealthy will go to save money. The incident underscored the disconnect between the public and their elected officials, fueling the perception that politicians often live by different rules. Amid the uproar, Kerry promptly agreed to pay the overdue taxes. Still, the episode remains a memorable example of the financial shenanigans that can trap even the most prominent political figures.

Grab Bag of Useless Helpful Tidbits

1. **Salaries of Politicians**: In the U.S., the President earns $400,000 annually (as of 2024), while Senators and Representatives make $174,000 annually. These figures don't include the myriad perks and benefits of the positions.
2. **Wealthiest Politicians**: Some of the wealthiest U.S. politicians include Michael Bloomberg, with a net worth exceeding $60 billion, and Nancy Pelosi, with assets reportedly in the tens of millions.
3. **Campaign Finances**: Running for office is a costly endeavor. The 2020 U.S. presidential election saw candidates spending billions, with Joe Biden's campaign raising over $1 billion.
4. **Financial Disclosures**: Politicians must file financial disclosure reports, but these often reveal surprising or dubious sources of income, leading to public skepticism about their integrity.
5. **Perks and Benefits**: In addition to their salaries, politicians receive benefits like pensions, healthcare, and travel allowances. Former presidents also receive a pension and funds for office staff and travel.
6. **Post-Political Careers**: Many politicians turn to lucrative careers after leaving office, becoming lobbyists, corporate consultants, or media personalities. Bill Clinton, for example, has earned millions in speaking fees.
7. **Economic Backgrounds**: Politicians' economic backgrounds can influence their policy decisions. For instance, wealthy politicians may prioritize tax cuts and deregulation, while those from humble beginnings might focus on social welfare programs.
8. **Impact on Policy**: Personal wealth and financial interests often shape political decisions. Politicians with significant investments may push for policies that benefit their financial portfolios.
9. **Rampant Corruption**: The public perception of politics is rife with

accusations of corruption. Scandals involving bribery, embezzlement, and fraud frequently make headlines, reinforcing the idea that politics is "a racket."

10. **Public Perception**: Many Americans view politics as "rigged" or "a scam." Polls regularly show low trust in government, with many believing that politicians are primarily self-serving.

11. **Lobbying Influence**: Lobbying is a billion-dollar industry, with corporations and special interest groups spending vast sums to influence legislation. This practice fuels public cynicism about whose interests politicians genuinely serve.

12. **Revolving Door**: The "revolving door" phenomenon, where politicians and regulators move between public office and private sector jobs, raises concerns about conflicts of interest and undue influence.

13. **Wealth Disparity**: The disparity between politicians and average citizens is stark. This gap can lead to policies that favor the affluent, exacerbating income inequality and eroding public trust.

14. **Financial Scandals**: Financial scandals are a staple in politics. From the Teapot Dome scandal in the 1920s to more recent events like the Panama Papers, these incidents highlight the ongoing issues of corruption and illicit financial practices.

15. **Ethics Violations**: Ethics violations, such as insider trading and campaign funds misuse, are common. These violations further damage the public's perception of the integrity of their elected officials.

16. **Wealthiest Congress Members**: The U.S. Congress has many millionaires. In 2019, over half of the members of Congress were millionaires, a stark contrast to the general population.

17. **Self-Funding Campaigns**: Wealthy politicians often use personal funds to finance their campaigns, giving them a significant advantage over less affluent opponents and raising questions about money's influence in politics.

18. **Financial Transparency**: Despite financial disclosure requirements, many loopholes allow politicians to obscure the full extent of their wealth and financial dealings.

19. **Public Skepticism**: The constant flow of financial scandals and ethical breaches contributes to a pervasive skepticism among the public. Many believe that politicians are out of touch with the realities faced by ordinary citizens.

20. **"Politics as a Joke"**: Comedians and satirists often highlight the absurdities and contradictions in political life, reinforcing the idea that politics is "a joke." Shows like "The Daily Show" and "Last Week Tonight" thrive on this public sentiment.

Great Big Grab Bag of Fun Factoids

1. **Richest Presidents**: George Washington was among the wealthiest U.S. presidents, with an estimated net worth of $580 million (adjusted for inflation), mainly due to his extensive land holdings.

2. **Senate Millionaires**: As of 2019, over half of the U.S. Senate were millionaires, with some members like Mitt Romney and Mark Warner having fortunes exceeding $100 million.

3. **Notable Financial Scandals**: The Watergate scandal involved political espionage and illicit campaign finances, leading to widespread distrust in government.

4. **Amusing Financial Disclosures**: Former U.S. Senator Al Franken once joked in his financial disclosure that he had a check for $50 from a comedy club that had never been cashed, illustrating the sometimes-absurd nature of these reports.

5. **Politicians' Side Hustles**: Some politicians have had unusual side jobs. For example, former Congressman Sonny Bono continued to earn royalties from his music career while serving in office, blending entertainment with politics.

This chapter showcases the intricate and often murky economics of political life, revealing the financial realities and public perceptions that shape the political landscape.

Your Great Big Grab Bag of Useless Trivia: American Politics

1. Filibustering Follies

Did you know that the longest filibuster in U.S. Senate history was conducted by Strom Thurmond in 1957? He spoke for 24 hours and 18 minutes in an attempt to block the Civil Rights Act of 1957. Armed with throat lozenges, a steam bath before his marathon, and a prepared bladder (thanks to trips to the Senate sauna to dehydrate himself), Thurmond's effort was as futile as it was lengthy. The bill passed anyway.

2. The Furry Candidates

In the 2016 presidential election, a cat named Limberbutt McCubbins ran for president. Registered as a Democrat, Limberbutt's platform was based on the idea of a "perfect" administration. While he didn't win, his campaign highlighted the absurdity of the election process, and he certainly won the internet's heart.

3. Dueling for Honor

Alexander Hamilton and Aaron Burr's famous duel in 1804 wasn't the only time politicians took their grievances to the field of honor. Dueling was a common way to settle political disputes in the early Republic. Andrew Jackson, for instance, participated in numerous duels, one of which left a bullet permanently lodged near his heart.

4. The Dead Voter Society

Chicago is notorious for its history of election fraud, particularly the claim that the dead voted in large numbers during the 1960 presidential election. While the extent of this fraud is debated, it's a testament to the lengths some will go to sway political outcomes. "Vote early, vote often," indeed!

5. Congressional Cage Matches

In 1856, Representative Preston Brooks of South Carolina famously caned Senator Charles Sumner of Massachusetts on the Senate floor. This violent outburst was in response to Sumner's anti-slavery speech, demonstrating that political discourse wasn't always limited to sharp words—sometimes, it involved sharp blows.

6. Presidential Pets with Power

Calvin Coolidge's menagerie at the White House included a pygmy hippo named Billy, a gift from rubber magnate Harvey Firestone. Billy's presence and the other exotic animals Coolidge received brought a unique atmosphere to the White House, blending political power with wild curiosity.

7. Write-In Wonders

1932, a peculiar situation occurred in Athens, Tennessee, where the city council race was held. After a contentious election, a goat was elected via a write-in campaign. The goat, known as Clay Henry, symbolizes the town's frustration with the corruption and ineptitude of human candidates.

8. Campaign Promises Gone Wild

In 1968, comedian Pat Paulsen ran a satirical campaign for president with the slogan, "I've upped my standards, now up yours." His campaign poked fun at the political process, highlighting the absurdity of many campaign promises. Paulsen's platform included outlawing the human race and a pledge to stop the Cold War and start a hot one.

9. The Incumbent Advantage

James Michael Curley, a mayor of Boston, was so beloved by his constituents that he was re-elected while serving a prison sentence for mail fraud. Curley ran his campaign from his cell, proving that being behind bars isn't necessarily a barrier to holding office for some politicians.

10. The Duel for the Duel

In 1806, Andrew Jackson dueled with Charles Dickinson, a duel known for its bloodiness and personal nature. Dickinson accused Jackson's wife of bigamy, leading to a fatal encounter where Jackson was shot in the chest but managed to return fire, killing Dickinson. Jackson's survival and reputation for toughness were cemented that day.

11. The Swing of Things

In the early 19th century, the House of Representatives was so chaotic that it required a sergeant-at-arms to carry a mace as a symbol of order. On one occasion, John Quincy Adams had to brandish the mace to restore calm during a particularly unruly session.

12. Teddy's Big Stick

Theodore Roosevelt's "Big Stick" ideology wasn't just a political metaphor. He was known for his physical vigor, once giving a 90-minute speech after being shot in an assassination attempt. The bullet, slowed by a glasses case and a thick manuscript in his pocket, stayed in his chest as he spoke, embodying his fearless approach to leadership.

13. The Anti-Masonic Party

In 1828, America saw the rise of its first third party—the Anti-Masonic Party. Formed in response to the mysterious disappearance of William Morgan, who was allegedly murdered for revealing Masonic secrets, the party capitalized on public fear and suspicion of secret societies.

14. The Candy Desk

Since 1965, the "Candy Desk" has been a tradition in the U.S. Senate. It's located near the entrance, with sweets for senators to snack on. Various senators have occupied the desk over the years, each continuing the sugary tradition and providing a literal sweet spot in the halls of power.

15. Quirky Quorums

The Texas Legislature once faced a quorum crisis when opposing party members fled to Oklahoma to avoid voting on a redistricting plan. Known as the "Texas Eleven," these Democratic state senators' absence stalled the legislative process and highlighted the extreme lengths politicians will go to block legislation.

16. The Kingfish's Kingdom

Huey Long, Louisiana's infamous governor and senator, ran the state with an iron fist and a flair for the dramatic. His political machine was so powerful that he once declared, "I am the Constitution around here." Long's populist policies and autocratic style left an indelible mark on Louisiana politics.

17. Pork Barrel Politics

"Pork barrel" projects refer to government spending for localized projects secured solely to bring money to a representative's district. The term dates back to the 19th century, when barrels of salt pork were a common form of sustenance. These projects often lead to accusations of wasteful spending but remain a staple of legislative maneuvering.

18. The Velvet Hammer

Nancy Pelosi, the first female Speaker of the House, earned the nickname "The Velvet Hammer" for her ability to combine a personable approach with formidable political acumen. Her tenure has been marked by significant legislative achievements and a reputation for keeping her party in line.

19. The War on Squirrels

In 1987, the White House grounds faced an invasion—not of political rivals, but of squirrels. The furry creatures were causing havoc by chewing through electrical wires, leading to a "war" declared by the Reagan administration. The effort to control the squirrel population was part of the quirky behind-the-scenes life at 1600 Pennsylvania Avenue.

20. The Political Pardon

One of the most controversial presidential pardons was Gerald Ford's pardon of Richard Nixon following the Watergate scandal. The decision, aimed at healing the nation, was highly contentious and is often debated as either a necessary step for moving forward or a grave injustice.

21. The Floating Capitol

During the War of 1812, British forces set fire to Washington, D.C., leading to the hurried evacuation of government documents and officials. The Library of Congress's collection was almost destroyed, prompting Thomas Jefferson to sell his library to the government to restart the collection.

22. The Blind Trust

Lyndon B. Johnson was known for his larger-than-life personality and intimidating "Johnson Treatment," a mix of persuasion and pressure. He once convinced a senator to support a bill by cornering him in a Capitol restroom, leaning in close, and using his imposing stature to make his case.

23. The Human Blockade

In 2013, Senator Ted Cruz performed a 21-hour filibuster against the Affordable Care Act, famously reading "Green Eggs and Ham" by Dr. Seuss. While technically not a filibuster in the traditional sense, Cruz's marathon speech aimed to rally conservative opposition and drew national attention.

24. Presidential Pets: Part II

Herbert Hoover's Belgian Shepherd, King Tut, was credited with helping him win the 1928 election. Hoover's campaign utilized photos of him with the dog to soften his image and appeal to the public's love of pets. King Tut even had his campaign slogan: "A Vote for Hoover is a Vote for King Tut!"

25. The Senator's Sneaker

Alfonse D'Amato, a senator from New York, earned the nickname "Senator Pothole" for his attention to constituent services, famously responding to local concerns, including filling potholes. This hands-on approach endeared him to voters and showcased the importance of addressing everyday political issues.

26. The Phantom Voter

In 1948, the Democratic primary for the U.S. Senate in Texas saw a mysterious turn of events when 202 additional ballots were found in Precinct 13, all favoring Lyndon B. Johnson. This discovery led to his razor-thin victory and earned him the nickname "Landslide Lyndon," a reminder of the murky waters of election integrity.

27. The Sitting Bull

In 1946, the Republican Party gained control of Congress and placed a "bull" (a symbolic figure) in a prominent position in the House chamber to signify their dominance. The bull remained a reminder of the power shift and the political symbolism often accompanying legislative victories.

28. Presidential Ghosts

The White House is said to be haunted by several ghosts, including that of Abraham Lincoln. Numerous presidents, including Harry Truman and Winston Churchill (while visiting), reported eerie encounters with Lincoln's spirit. The ghostly presence adds a layer of supernatural intrigue to America's most famous residence.

29. The Senate Bean Soup

The Senate has served bean soup in its dining room for over a century, regardless of the season. The tradition started in the early 1900s and continues today, offering a comforting and constant culinary reminder of the Senate's storied past.

30. The Mispronounced Name

Former Vice President Spiro Agnew's unusual name often led to mispronunciations and ridicule. Johnny Carson once quipped that Agnew sounded like "a town in Norway" or "a rare gas." Despite the jokes, Agnew's name remains one of the most distinctive in American political history.

31. The Accidental President

Gerald Ford is the only person to become president without being elected to the presidency or vice presidency. Appointed vice president after Spiro Agnew's resignation and ascending to the presidency after Nixon's resignation, Ford's path to the Oval Office was as unprecedented as it was unusual.

32. The Iconic Hat

Abraham Lincoln's stovepipe hat wasn't just a fashion statement but a practical accessory. Lincoln often used his hat to store important documents and notes, making it a mobile filing cabinet. The hat has since become an iconic symbol of his presidency and unique approach to personal organization.

33. The Canine Candidate

In 1984, a dog named Bosco won the mayoral election in Sunol, California. The black Labrador-Rottweiler mix served as the town's unofficial mayor, embodying the quirky charm of small-town politics. Bosco's tenure was marked by good-natured governance and a focus on community spirit.

34. The Political Parrot

Andrew Jackson's pet parrot, Poll, was known for its colorful vocabulary, which unfortunately included a repertoire of curse words. The parrot's outbursts were so notorious that it had to be removed from Jackson's funeral for swearing too much, leaving a lasting impression on the guests.

35. The Whig Party Woes

The Whig Party, active in the mid-19th century, was so divided on critical issues like slavery that it eventually collapsed. The infighting and lack of a unified stance on crucial matters led to the party's dissolution, paving the way for the rise of the Republican Party.

36. The Big Cheese

In 1837, President Andrew Jackson received a 1,400-pound block of cheese as a gift from a New York dairy farmer. Jackson kept it in the White House foyer, and the pungent smell had permeated the building by the time he left office. Martin Van Buren's successor held a public "cheese feast" to eliminate it.

37. The Secret Swearing-In

Lyndon B. Johnson was sworn in as president aboard Air Force One just hours after JFK's assassination. The hurried ceremony took place in Dallas with a borrowed Bible, marking one of American history's most abrupt and somber transitions of power.

38. The Prohibition Proponents

The temperance movement, which led to Prohibition in 1920, was strongly supported by various politicians and activists who believed alcohol was the root of social ills. However, the unintended consequences of prohibition, such as the rise of organized crime, eventually led to its repeal in 1933.

39. The Pardon Power

President Jimmy Carter's pardon of Vietnam War draft evaders in 1977 was a controversial use of presidential pardon power. The decision aimed at national reconciliation, but it sparked significant debate about justice and forgiveness in the context of wartime actions.

40. The Mullet Manifesto

During the 2020 presidential campaign, Joe Exotic (of "Tiger King" fame) ran for president as an independent candidate. His platform, outlined in his "Mullet Manifesto," focused on exotic animal rights and personal freedoms. Although his candidacy was more spectacle than serious bid, it highlighted the eccentricities of American politics.

41. The Insect Infestation

In 1979, the White House faced an infestation of stink bugs. The Carter administration had to deal with the pervasive problem, a minor but persistent nuisance. The incident underscored that even the highest office in the land isn't immune to everyday annoyances.

42. The Unwanted Gift

In 1992, Ross Perot's presidential campaign received a peculiar gift: a live cow. The cow was intended to symbolize Perot's down-to-earth appeal and connection to rural America. While the gesture was well-meaning, it also highlighted political symbolism's quirky and sometimes bizarre nature.

43. The Banana Republic

The term "banana republic" was popularized by American writer O. Henry in the early 20th century to describe unstable countries in Central America with economies dependent on exporting bananas. The phrase has since been used to criticize political corruption and instability in various contexts.

44. The Great Emancipator's Beard

Abraham Lincoln decided to grow his famous beard after receiving a letter from 11-year-old Grace Bedell, who suggested that whiskers would improve his appearance and help him get elected. Lincoln took her advice, and the beard became one of his most recognizable features.

45. The Dual Officeholder

William Wirt, the U.S. Attorney General from 1817 to 1829, simultaneously served as the president of the American Colonization Society. His dual roles reflected early American politicians' overlapping responsibilities and interests, who often juggled multiple positions.

46. The Mysterious Disappearance

The disappearance of labor leader Jimmy Hoffa in 1975 remains one of America's greatest mysteries. While not a politician himself, Hoffa's connections to influential figures and organized crime have fueled endless speculation about his fate and the involvement of political entities.

47. The First Female Candidate

Victoria Woodhull was the first woman to run for U.S. president in 1872, representing the Equal Rights Party. Her candidacy was groundbreaking, though she faced significant opposition and legal challenges, including arrest for "obscenity" just days before the election.

48. The Grizzly Governor

In 2003, Arnold Schwarzenegger, known for his roles in action films, was elected governor of California in a recall election. His celebrity status and larger-than-life persona brought a unique dynamic to California politics, blending Hollywood glamour with state governance.

49. The Twin Presidents

The only U.S. president to have a twin was George H.W. Bush. His twin brother, Prescott, was not as publicly known but shared a close bond with the future president. This familial connection added an exciting facet to the Bush political dynasty.

50. The First Presidential Impeachment

Andrew Johnson was the first U.S. president to be impeached in 1868 for violating the Tenure of Office Act. His impeachment trial highlighted the intense political battles of the Reconstruction era and set a precedent for the legal and political process of impeachment.

51. The "Chicken War"

In 1962, the United States and European Economic Community engaged in a trade dispute known as the "Chicken War." The conflict arose over tariffs on American poultry, leading to retaliatory tariffs on European goods, including light trucks, which still affect the auto industry today.

52. Presidential Baseball

President George H.W. Bush was a skilled first baseman and captain of the Yale baseball team. He played in the first two College World Series and even met Babe Ruth during college, fostering a lifelong love for the sport.

53. The "Hot Dog Summit"

1939, President Franklin D. Roosevelt hosted a "hot dog summit" for the British King and Queen. This informal picnic at Hyde Park introduced the royal guests to American cuisine and was a significant moment in U.S.-UK relations before World War II.

54. First Presidential Film Appearance

President Woodrow Wilson was the first sitting U.S. president to appear in a film. In 1915, he screened the controversial movie "The Birth of a Nation" at the White House, a decision that sparked significant debate and criticism due to the film's racist content.

55. Capitol Crypt

The U.S. Capitol building has a crypt intended to house the tomb of George Washington. However, Washington was never buried there, as he wished to be interred at his Mount Vernon estate. The crypt now serves as a museum and a fascinating historical oddity within the Capitol.

Recap of Highlights

From filibusters to furry candidates, American politics is a rich tapestry of bizarre, intriguing, and often humorous anecdotes. We've explored the longest filibuster by Strom Thurmond, the unlikely presidential run of a cat named Limberbutt McCubbins, and the notorious duel between Alexander Hamilton and Aaron Burr. We've delved into the history of ghostly encounters in the White House, the antics of presidential pets, and the peculiarities of election fraud claims. The whimsical tales of Andrew Jackson's duels, Calvin Coolidge's exotic pets, and the "Texas Eleven" fleeing the state add to the colorful narrative of American political history.

Further Exploration

American politics is full of fascinating stories and complex dynamics extending beyond the quirky trivia this book covers. To truly appreciate the depth and breadth of political history and its current implications, consider diving deeper into specific topics of interest. There is always more to learn and understand, whether it's the evolution of political parties, the intricacies of legislative processes, or the biographies of influential political figures. Engage with various resources, stay informed about current events, and continue to explore the multifaceted world of American politics.

Additional Resources

For those eager to dive deeper into the complexities and curiosities of American politics, here are some recommended books, websites, and other resources:

Books

1. **"Team of Rivals: The Political Genius of Abraham Lincoln" by Doris Kearns Goodwin**
    - A detailed account of Lincoln's leadership and relationship with his cabinet members.
2. **"The Federalist Papers" by Alexander Hamilton, James Madison, and John Jay**
    - Essential reading for understanding the foundational ideas of the U.S. Constitution.
3. **"Fear and Loathing on the Campaign Trail '72" by Hunter S. Thompson**
    - A gonzo journalist's perspective on the 1972 presidential campaign.
4. **"The Best and the Brightest" by David Halberstam**
    - An exploration of the Kennedy and Johnson administration's handling of the Vietnam War.
5. **"What You Should Know About Politics . . . But Don't: A Nonpartisan Guide to the Issues That Matter" by Jessamyn Conrad**
    - an excellent primer for anyone looking to understand the critical issues in American politics.

Websites

1. **Congress.gov**[1]
    - Official site for U.S. federal legislative information.
2. **Politico**[2]

---

1. https://www.congress.gov/

- ◦ A leading source for political news and analysis.
3. **FiveThirtyEight**[3]
   - ◦ Data-driven coverage of politics and election forecasts.
4. **FactCheck.org**[4]
   - ◦ A non-partisan site that monitors the factual accuracy of statements by political figures.
5. **The National Archives**[5]
   - ◦ A treasure trove of historical documents and resources on U.S. government and history.

Other Resources

1. **C-SPAN**
   - ◦ Watch live and recorded coverage of federal government proceedings and public affairs programming.
2. **Library of Congress**
   - ◦ Explore vast collections of books, manuscripts, and documents about American history and politics.
3. **National Constitution Center**
   - ◦ Interactive exhibits and educational resources focused on the U.S. Constitution.

---

2. https://www.politico.com/

3. https://fivethirtyeight.com/

4. https://www.factcheck.org/

5. https://www.archives.gov/

Did you love *555 Reasons to Roll Your Eyes at American Politics*? Then you should read *How to Understand Left-Wing Political Spin*[6] by Michael P. Clutton!

Unmask Liberal Narratives and Decipher the Absurdities of Political Spin.

Are you ready to cut through the fog of political spin and liberal myths? "How to Understand Left-Wing Political Spin" is here to demystify the complexities of political narratives and give you the factual insight to see through the often-confusing world of politics.

In this engaging exposé, a reluctant genius explains the intricacies of political spin and debunks the liberal myths that dominate the media. You'll decipher the tactics used in left-wing political narratives and gain the clarity needed to develop your own well-informed opinions, instead of simply accepting mass media talking points. From humorous anecdotes to hard-hitting, verifiable facts, your new favorite genius peels back the layers of the political onion in a way that appeals to both sides of the aisle.

---

6. https://books2read.com/u/3LlrND

7. https://books2read.com/u/3LlrND

Uncover the truth behind left-wing political spin and liberal myths. With each chapter, you'll slice through the political narratives that shape public opinion. To better understand the nuances of our ridiculous political concepts, you'll be more confident in your ability to properly communicate your viewpoint. And, brace yourself, you'll soon be able to debunk the common misconceptions your misinformed friends still assume are valid. Who knew you could be so politically correct—literally.

Equip yourself with the knowledge to explain and decipher political spin, and never be swayed by misleading narratives again. The full scope of left-wing strategies and liberal myths doesn't have to corrupt your life the way it does the mainstream media. This is a must-read for anyone who still wants to enjoy free will. Who cares what the celebrities tell you to do? After reading this provocative book, you'll see through the smoke and mirrors of political discourse and be almost as smart as the genius who wrote it.

Read more at www.michaelpclutton.com.

Also by Michael Clutton

Hooked On Reel Fishing
How to Tackle Saltwater Fishing
Big Game Fishing
Off Shore Fishing Adventures

The Juice Chronicles
Bloodlines: The Juice Chronicles

Your Great Big Grab Bag of Useless Helpful Tidbits
Charity Giving Donation Revelation
555 Reasons to Roll Your Eyes at American Politics

Watch for more at www.michaelpclutton.com.

Also by Michael P. Clutton

Secrets of a Reluctant Genius
How to Understand Left-Wing Political Spin

Your Great Big Grab Bag of Useless Helpful Tidbits
Religions of the World
555 Reasons to Roll Your Eyes at American Politics

Standalone
Echoes of Reality

Watch for more at www.michaelpclutton.com.

About the Author

Michael P. Clutton isn't your typical storyteller. Since he was young, he loved drawing cartoons and writing stories, which not only kept him busy but also helped him learn more words. This early passion for fiction laid the foundation for his unique voice—rich, imaginative, and brimming with wit.

Michael's sarcastic and unique perspective on life adds intrigue to his daily routine and captivates those around him. Known for his quick wit and self-deprecating humor, he can generate a giggle or a guffaw at the drop of a hat. His creative toolbox is well-stocked with both artwork and the written word, making him a versatile and dynamic creator.

Discover the captivating world of Michael P. Clutton, an author who combines humor, heart, and a deep passion for creativity in his stories and art.

Read more at www.michaelpclutton.com.